Our Wars Overseas And At Home

VILNIUS – DRESDEN – NEW YORK – DA NANG – TAM KY POTSDAM – SANTO DOMINGO

Observations, Analysis and Themes
It is the highest honor and privilege to serve our country.

Also Author of the book
From Immigrant To U.S. Marine

LtCol Dominik George Nargele USMC (Ret)

authorHOUSE®

AuthorHouse™
1663 Liberty Drive
Bloomington, IN 47403
www.authorhouse.com
Phone: 833-262-8899

Published by AuthorHouse 08/09/2023

ISBN: 978-1-4259-8347-5 (sc)
ISBN: 978-1-4259-9909-4 (hc)

Print information available on the last page.

ACKNOWLEDGMENTS

A special thanks must go to the distinguished reviewers of the draft manuscript of this book and their insightful comments, General P. X. Kelley USMC (Ret); Ambassador Lev E. Dobriansky; Ambassador William A. Brown; Lieutenant General Stephen Olmstead USMC (Ret); Major General Donald R. Gardner USMC (Ret), President of the Marine Corps University; Father Francis Giedgautas, OFM; Major General W. H. Rice USMC (Ret); Brigadier General Edwin H. Simmons USMC (Ret); Charles Krutz, SES (Ret); Colonel William K. Rockey USMC (Ret); Colonel Frederick C. Turner USA (Ret); Captain Charles Chadbourn USNR, Naval War College; Colonel John Keenan USMC (Ret), Editor, Marine Corps Gazette; Colonel Paul Nikulla USAF (Ret); Colonel L. G. Kelley USMC (Ret); Colonel James Quisenberry USMC (Ret); Colonel William V. Bournes USA (Ret); Bebe F. Rice, Author; Trudy Wilkinson; Lieutenant Colonel Con Silard USMC (Ret); Lieutenant Colonel Douglas Guiler USA (Ret); Lieutenant Colonel Russell Lloyd, Jr. USMC (Ret); Lieutenant Colonel Frank Kelly USMC (Ret); Lieutenant Colonel Robert J. Metzger USA (Ret); Lieutenant Colonel Paul Grant USA (Ret.); Major Franklin Broadwell USMC (Ret); Elizabeth R. Birkhimer; Gediminas Indreika; Jurate Micuta and Patricia Snellings.

Thanks to family and friends for their help and comments, Cynthia, Jana and Rocky Meskauskas; Ella Waller Nargele; Nora and Tim Cullen; Lelia Belle Waller; Karen and Eric Meskauskas; Elaine Gardner; Audrey and Lacy Powell; Britton Warfield and Virginia Morgan. Ultimately, I am responsible for the contents and any errors.

Thanks to Marel Mallari for her help with the preparation of this manuscript.
Copyright Library of Congress 2005 161662
Dominik George Nargele
P.O. Box 4396
Arlington, VA 22204-0396

This book is most respectfully dedicated
to the Victims of Communism and Terror,
and to the Freedom and Independence of all
Captive Nations and People.

TABLE OF CONTENTS

CHAPTER 1 –
INTRODUCTION

BACKGROUND, OUR CONSTITUTION AND
REMEMBERING THE BUREAU OF CENSORSHIP

When taking the oath of office during commissioning ceremonies, I solemnly swore to uphold and defend the Constitution against all enemies foreign and domestic. It seemed that the foreign enemies were, in general terms, Communist police state mass murderers, fanatic Islamic sect totalitarians and the members of deadly criminal enterprises. All foreign enemies were fighting against freedom. It was much less clear to me, who the domestic enemies were and what they were fighting for.

The First Amendment of our Constitution gives us the right of freedom of speech, however, freedom of speech, in my opinion, does not give us, our media, our politicians and our special interests, permission to stab Americans who are fighting overseas in the back and to support our enemies. Section 3 of our Constitution states that treason against the United States shall consist in levying war against them, or in adhering to their enemies, giving them aid and comfort. It can be argued that during the War on Terror, just as during the Vietnam war, some persons have undermined the war effort while propagating their own agenda. It is common knowledge that many in our media, academia and among special interest groups lean left. They slant their reporting, lectures and funding to benefit liberal politicians who claim that war is not the answer. Some want to make love not war, with the latest gang of ruthless killers, who are trying to murder their way to power.

Whereas we have the right to our opinions and to talk freely about politics, our freedom of speech and expression does not include hampering our national defense at the time of war. We are truly at war against global terrorists, yet a Fifth Column of media and political activists seem to sometimes undermine our war efforts. The activists feed off each other with outlandish claims and allegations, while our enemies are often given inside information by journalists and those who leak secrets about our vulnerabilities and successes. Terrorists are given access to insights and the knowledge of experts about our conduct of the war. By promoting their agenda, some politicians and journalists inadvertently support our enemies by claiming that we are losing the war, are in a quagmire and in a civil war.

1

According to a writer who worked with an educational consulting firm in Illinois, some politicians apparently aided our enemies before the War on Terror in the past. In 1970, John Kerry conducted a meeting with North Vietnamese Communists despite laws which forbid private citizens from negotiating with foreign powers. Mr. Kerry gave a press conference advocating the North Vietnamese peace plan in which our country would have had to pay reparations and agree that we lost the war. According to Grove City College professor Paul Kengor's book, "The Crusader Ronald Reagan and the Fall of Communism", a 14 May 1983 letter from the KGB head Viktor Chebrikov to Soviet leader Yuri Andropov stated that Senator Edward Kennedy had contacted the Soviets and wanted to collaborate with the KGB before our 1984 elections, to arm Soviet officials regarding explanations for nuclear disarmament problems and to influence Americans with televised Andropov interviews in the USA.

Senator Edward Kennedy and some other politicians, have undermined our leaders by accusing them of fabricating data (to justify the War on Terror) and by making outlandish demands. If the President were to cave in to the many demands to fire civilian leaders and precipitously withdraw our troops, it would disrupt military operations and put our country at greater risk in my opinion. We have unique laws that guarantee our right to life, liberty and the pursuit of happiness but we are at war against global terrorists. It seems that some of our politicians, members of our media and our special interest groups have sometimes aided our enemies at the time of war in the name of free speech and the right to descent.

Upon retirement, I was told by superiors that now I could say something about our wars overseas and at home. What I wanted to say was that I was sometimes concerned while serving overseas about people at home who seemingly supported our enemies. Some clear examples from the past are, Dexter White, the Rosenbergs and Alger Hiss, now confirmed domestic enemies by declassified official documents of the Soviet Union, despite objections by American activists. Other examples which come to mind are, the cases of Aldrich Ames and Robert Hansen. Both greatly aided the Soviet Union during the Cold War while we were fighting against Communism. Also, an attractive young lady, Ana Montes, who was given a high paying job as a defense analyst and access to almost all top secret information in Washington, decided one day to turn it all over to the Cuban Communists out of sympathy for them. She met with Cuban agents twice a week for a number of years to help the Communists before she was discovered. Then, a former national security advisor, Samuel Berger, reportedly has concealed evidence of derelections by President Bill Clinton or his aides about terrorist activities in America prior to 9/11.

According to Michael Barone and his recent article, "Our Covert Enemies", our many domestic enemies in the war against Terror and Communism are both overt foreign and covert domestic. The aims of overt foreign enemies are clearly to force our submission to their totalitarian ideology by violent means and acts of terror. It seems to me that we generally know who many of the terrorists are and where they come from. Our covert enemies are much harder to recognize since they live among us in large numbers in different places of our society. They enjoy our free lifestyles, our many benefits and demand even more benefits and freedoms.

Our covert enemies appear to have no explicit desire to destroy everything but instead have been working over the years to undermine our laws, beliefs and institutions on which our society is based. Some covert enemies are among our elites who have promoted moral relativism, multiculturalism and transnationalism. Transnationalism allows the flying of foreign flags, foreign demonstrations, open borders and the colonization of parts of our country by foreigners. During the Vietnam War, some of our pro-Communist activists were openly flying enemy flags on Capitol Hill and associated with enemy diplomats and agents as part of the anti-war movement. An executive order, issued by President Bill Clinton, later declared that your language is that of the country of your origin, causing law suits against our institutions for failing to provide translations in any of 500 languages.

According to moral relativism, no ideology is superior to another. Consequently, it is held that dictators like Stalin, Ho Chi Minh, Fidel Castro and Saddam Hussein had their ways, we have ours and who is to say who is right. No ideas should be "privileged", especially those which have produced Western civilization. For example, the founding principle of Roman and Western law called "pater familius" which states that the father is the head of the family should be changed. History which describes the greatness of the Roman empire, Western civilization, Europe's achievements in science and the arts, should be rewriten eliminating the "dead white men" like Tacitus, Newton, Bach and Einstein. Rich white men have imposed their ideas on benighted people of color around the world and are morally stained and wrong, according to moral relativists who affirmed that all societies are equal but ours is even worse than equal because of our heritage and leadership. The idea that one culture could possible be superior to another is considered to be intolerant and violates the liberal values of moral relativists.

The principles of moral relativism, multiculturalism and transnationalism have been propagated by some elites in America for decades. In the 1960s, the young elite men who refused to serve in the Armed Forces during the Vietnam War and the Cold War, set out to establish moral relative arguments that they and those who deserted our country during times of war were heroes, rather than those who obeyed the call to duty. President Jimmy Carter then pardoned the deserters while apparently performing other acts of disservice to our country, such as overthrowing the Shah of Iran and ushering in the Islamic fundamentalists who have been waging proxy wars and inciting 1.3 billion Muslims to conduct a Holy War against the Free World. Our elite activists and covert enemies have propagated their ideas through higher education and main stream media to the point that their relativisms of law, education, religion and politics have permeated the assumptions of millions. Our covert activists apparently do not want the terrorists to win but at the same time it seems that they would like to see us lose the War on Terror at home just as we lost the Vietnam War at home.

According to the journalist and author, Bernard Goldberg, the 110 people who have hurt America most during the War on Terror, are in different categories. The movie producer Michael Moore, who reportedly produced a "lie" according to former New York City Mayor Ed Koch and others, is reportedly being sued by Sergeant Peter Damons, who claims that Moore misrepresented him and the purpose of some of the photography. Moore has called the Iraqi terrorists "Minutemen" and Cindy Sheehan, not to be outdone, has called an American President "the world's greatest terrorist". A well known television anchor, Dan Rather, reportedly used documents which were not authenticated against the President's character and military service, until finally CBS retracted the allegations and apparently took administrative career action against Rather. The actress, Jane Fonda, has been seen by Vietnam veterans and other groups for decades as a domestic enemy, although many people still like her and she has been very successful in her profession. Her ex-husband, Ted Turner, stated in a television interview that we should withdraw from the Middle East and reduce our support to Israel. Also, Mr. George Soros, the chairman of his Open Society Institute, stated during a September 2006 television interview that the war against terrorists should be repudiated. As a new immigrant from Europe, he showed his gratitude for being allowed to come to America, by stating that he supports a stronger and more united Europe to counter-balance the USA. Furthermore, in 2004, he spent $27.5 million of his financial market made fortune against the President of the United States of America.

On 17 August 2006, Detroit District Judge Anna Diggs Taylor, a liberal activist judge appointed by President Jimmy Carter in 1979, struck down the NSA surveillance of terrorist program as unconstitutional. She not only gave a victory to the liberal American Civil Liberties Union (ACLU) which brought this foolish law suit before the court, but also to the terrorists by denigrating an essential tool in the War on Terror. The domestic surveillance program has helped to prevent terrorist attacks and saved American lives.

During World War II, domestic enemies were kept under control by the Bureau of Censorship and the FBI. Maybe we should do the same during the War on Terror. In my opinion, had we kept domestic enemies under better control during the Vietnam War, we might have won the Vietnam War not only overseas but also at home.

THE YALTA CONFERENCE AND DESTRUCTION OF DRESDEN

During the summer of 1968, the anti-war riots in Chicago at the Democratic Party Convention were described in the news media by some reporters as "America in a war against itself" and "the war at home". In addition to other episodes over the years, in June 2006, "the war on Capitol Hill" was reported to be ongoing about our Armed Forces in Iraq. In my opinion, the origins of many anti-war movements and civil unrest activities can be traced back in part to the end of World War II. On 4 February 1945, decisions were made at the Yalta Conference between President Franklin D. Roosevelt, Winston Churchill and Joseph Stalin which laid the foundation for many subsequent struggles and the Cold War.

The Cold War could be possibly described as World War III, since it lasted for nearly five decades and sometimes included high intensity combat for extended periods of time. It involved war in China, Europe, Korea, Latin America, Vietnam and the Middle East. The Global War on Terror is in some ways a continuation of past animosities with radical Islamic fanatics and terrorists assuming a major role with an alleged mission from God to destroy the free world. The Global War on Terror could be possibly described as World War IV because dirty bombs and nuclear weapons might possibly be used against our country and the free world, resulting in retaliation with even more powerful weapons by the U.S. and our allies. The Global War on Terror could be a new kind of war during which we may possibly expect dirty bombs and nuclear weapons to be delivered by unconventional means, such as in suit cases, ship containers or with shipments of illegal drugs.

At Yalta, Stalin reportedly demanded the destruction of German industrial and population centers by the British Royal Air Force and the U.S. Air Force. The Chief of the Soviet General Staff (STAVKA), General A.I. Antonov, presented a briefing in which the destruction of Dresden was demanded in order to facilitate the advance of the Soviet Army into Germany. President Roosevelt agreed to help destroy Dresden on 13 February 1945 among other targets. The Roosevelt administration accepted many additional Soviet demands because it was thought that the help of Stalin was needed to defeat Japan.

According to U.S. Air Force historians, about 25,000 persons were killed and 35,000 were wounded in Dresden during three days of bombing by the Royal and U.S. Air Forces. Some after-action assessments of casualties in Dresden were different and much higher. One study performed under contract for the U.S Army in Europe (USAEUR) by two former German Generals, came up with the highest total estimate of about 250,000. Maybe my family and I as a small child were included in the casualty count since the house we were staying in was hit by three incindiary gravity bombs. We subsequently were able to get out of the burning house and walked out of the burning city. We were Lithuanian refugees, trying to escape from Communism and the Soviet Army by fleeing to the West. Stalin had ordered the Soviet Army at that time, to kill all refugees fleeing from Communism, including women and children.

As it turned out later in 1945, America did not really need the help of the Soviet Union to fight against Japan. Japan surrendered on 14 August 1945 after President Harry Truman ordered the bombing of Hiroshima and Nagasaki but Stalin had already been given half of Europe, China, Northern Korea, Manchuria, North Vietnam and other territories by the Roosevelt administration. Reportedly President Roosevelt wanted to give half of Japan to Stalin also but General Douglas McArthur among others protested vehemently and saved post-war Japan from Communist enslavement and terror.

Our philosophy of appeasement, the apparent lack of foresight and diplomatic toughness at Yalta, were to haunt the American people for five decades to come. The price for the needless give-aways and appeasements to Stalin had to be paid for during the Cold War many times by Marines and soldiers with their lives during conflicts in Europe, China, Korea, Vietnam and the Middle East. The wars overseas were also marked by anti-war movements and civil unrest at home.

Whereas Stalin and his proteges, Mao Tse-tung, Kim Il Sung and Ho Chi Minh, executed those who failed to be politically correct, in America some Communist agents and their Cuban proxy representatives operated freely throughout our society. They operated with the support of our special interest groups, news media and wealthy moguls. The foreign agents, liberal politicians and reporters facilitated the conduct of wars at home and caused America to fight against itself while our Armed Forces were trying to defend our country overseas. According to a Wall Street Journal editor, we lost the Vietnam War because of a petty robbery in the Watergate apartment building, and the relentless attacks of the news media, politicians and interest groups at home against our country.

EVENTS LEADING TO THE RISE OF COMMUNISM

At the end of World War II in Europe, according to Anthony Beavor, the Soviet Army brought Communism and Stalin's dictatorship to Eastern and Central Europe as it advanced against the remnants of the German Army. More than seven million people fled westward during 1945 from the terror of the Soviet armed forces. In order to facilitate the escape of refugees, prisoners and displaced persons, German soldiers were holding off the Soviets in the east and giving ground to the American and British armies in the west. It was known in Europe that Stalin was ruthless and a mass-murderer. He was called by some Russians "the devil incarnate" because he slaughtered millions of people during his reign as the Chairman of the Central Committee of the Communist Party of the Soviet Union. President Ronald Reagan later called the Soviet super power which was created, an evil empire, as the rise of Communism took place everywhere in the world.

Middle class and educated Europeans in Central and Eastern Europe were turning to America for help but the Roosevelt Administration was helping Stalin not his victims. The seeds of conflict between the forces of freedom and democracy on one hand and Communist enslavement and terror on the other had been laid in the ashes of Europe. General George Patton understood Communism and according to a former member of his staff wanted to keep the Soviets from advancing in Czechoslovakia. General Patton was overruled by social democrats in Washington and London who supported Communism. A plan to destroy Central Europe and give everything possible to the Communists was reportedly developed by the Roosevelt administration. Those who wanted to rebuild Europe and establish democracy were in the minority and were shouted down. Colonel Lawrence Wilkinson, US Army (Reserve), who worked for General Lucius Clay in Berlin, described the hard fight to rebuild Germany to me many years later. Colonel Wilkinson volunteered to join the Army and served at a salary of one dollar per year. He subsequently was also the Civil Defense Director of New York.

At the end of World War II, Soviet Communists tried to disrupt all free democracies and take over the government of as many countries as they could. With the Soviet occupation of Eastern and Central Europe by the Soviet Army, came KGB and Ministry of the Interior units who conducted purges, executions and deportations now known as "ethnic cleansing". The Roosevelt administration helped the Communists in every way possible in order to secure the friendship of Stalin. According to American historian, Thomas Fleming, President Roosevelt told Stalin at Teharan that he could have Poland "just don't let the American voters know". Senator Barbara Mikulski (D-MD) stated many years later on public television, that after Roosevelt gave Poland to Stalin, her family placed President Roosevelt's picture face down on top of the fire place were it had been previously displayed in a place of honor.

Early in World War II, liberal Democrats in the Roosevelt administration demanded that Winston Churchill and the government of Great Britain dismantle the British Empire. In need of help from America, Great Britain was in no position to oppose President Roosevelt. Communist governments rushed in to take power where the British were forced to leave much earlier than they should have. The Communists took advantage of every opportunity created for them by inept American pro-left policies. With the support of liberal Democrats in Washington, the Soviets gained control in China and installed Mao Tsetung who mass-murdered about forty million people and initiated Communist infiltrations of all free democracies in Asia.

AIDING AND ABETTING THE COMMUNISTS

At the end of the World War II, famous Communists like Karl Marx, Lenin, Trotsky and Rosa Luxembourg where presented as models of world salvation at many American schools and were praised in many publications. Stalin continued to mass-murder Europeans by the millions and Mao Tsetung was doing the same in Asia. The Soviets conducted a campaign in 1945, to arrest and repatriate anti-Communist refugees in Europe with the help of the left-wing democracts in London and Washington. According to Anthony Beevor, the Communist forced repatriation process lasted until December 1946. About 5.5 million people were returned to the Soviet Union of which 1,833,567 had been prisoners of war. Most were sent to Soviet death camps and some to labor camps in Siberia to die in snow and ice.

Some well meaning and distinguished Americans, have aided the Communists since World War II without ever stopping to think what they were doing. One example, is the case of Willian Sloane Coffin, the former Yale University chaplain and activist against the Vietnam War. At the end of World War II, he served with the US Army as a Soviet and French liaison officer, taking part in the forced repatriation of refugees who were supposed "traitors" to Communism and did not want to return to Stalin's rule. Part of the Allied power's agreement with Stalin signed by the Roosevelt administration representatives called for "Operation Keelhaul" to take refugees back east by boxcar. Many were beaten in transit and were assured death by execution or in the GULAG (Glavnoye Upravleniye Lagerov).

A pivotal moment in Mr.Coffin's life, he wrote later in his memoir "Ounce to Every Man", was an invitation to a party among the refugees, who were unaware that they were being returned to Soviet control. "Several times I turned to the commandant (of the refugee camp) sitting next to me" to tip him off, he wrote. "Yet I couldn't bring myself to do it". When dawn broke and the refugees realized where they were being taken, Mr.Coffin witnessed a series of suicide attempts; one man rammed his head into a glass window and began sawing to cut his jugular vein. The scenes implanted a life-long burden on his conscience and led him, after earning his degree at Yale University, to join the Central Intelligence Agency to serve to oppose Stalin.

Nevertheless, Mr. Coffin along with Benjamin Spock and some others was subsequently convicted of conspiracy to aid and abet disobedience to the Selective Service Act. He then championed the termination of NATO and opposed the war in Vietnam in every way. It seems to me, Mr. Coffin did not understand that just as he helped Stalin kill innocent anti-Communist refugees in Europe so he helped Ho Chi Minh kill innocent anti-Communist refugees in Vietnam.

THE IDEALIZATION AND SUPPORT OF LEFT-WING DICTATORS AND TERRORISTS

In the American war against itself, the idealization by some Americans of left-wing dictators like Joseph Stalin, Mao Tse-tung, Kim Il Sung, Fidel Castro and others played a part. Some Americans combined the idealization and support for left-wing dictators with a deep hatred of their own country and the hatred of some American presidents. Probably the dictators who always wanted to do all possible harm to America must have marveled about how much anti-Americanism existed in our country.

In the late 1950s, as a graduate student at Columbia University I remember the great welcome and admiration for Fidel Castro and Che Guevarra at our school and in New York City. The main-stream news media idolized Fidel and his revolutionaries and many reporters praised him as the saviour of Cuba and the free world. For example, the famous woman reporter Dickey Chapelle, who was imprisoned by Communists during the 1956 Hungarian Revolution, became at first a Castro supporter. Although she was ardently anti-Communist after being imprisoned in Hungary for nearly two months, she gave Castro the benefit of a doubt about his pro-Communist activities.

Then in 1962, Dickey Chapelle began to change her mind about Fidel because of the Cuban Missile Crisis. I remember that while I was serving as a platoon leader, with Company H, 2nd Battalion, 6th Marines on the USS York County in the Mediterranean Sea, some criticisms appeared in newspapers about Fidel Castro and his Communist government after many Soviet style executions took place in Cuba. In September 1962, when the missile crisis broke out, my ship and many others were sent from the Mediterranean Sea to Cuban waters. The USS Enterprise, on which by the way, Lieutenant John

McCain USN was serving as a pilot, was with us in the Mediterranean Sea and got to Cuba ahead of our LST-1175, the USS York County. Many years later, it seemed interesting to me when Senator McCain talked about these events in an interview with historians and reporters on public television.

THE CUBAN MISSILE CRISIS OF 1962

In 1962, Fidel Castro had become a strong ally of the Soviet Union and allowed the Soviets to station missiles with nuclear warheads in Cuba. The Soviets then stationed troops in Cuba to operate and protect the missiles. They could blow away Miami, Atlanta or other cities in minutes and kill thousands of Americans, if the Kremlin leaders gave the order. President John F. Kennedy then quarantined Cuba and the greatest crisis of the Cold War had been precipitated with the help of Fidel Castro. Our company commander, Captain John Wiita with executive officer 1st Lieutenant E. T. Fitzgerald, 1st Sergeant Stiles and Gunnery Sergeant Subjanits, gave us orders to land on a beach near Havana and we were ready to go. It was my great honor and privilege to lead the first platoon. Our 2nd Platoon Leader was 2nd Lieutenant Donald R. Gardner, later Major General and President of the Marine Corps University. Our 3rd Platoon Leader was 2nd Lieutenant Pat Tatum and our Weapons Platoon Leader was 2nd Lieutenant Jack Scott. Fortunately, we did not have to land since Nikita Khrushchev gave in to our demands under enormous pressure and withdrew the Soviet nuclear missiles.

After the crisis, many adverse facts about Fidel Castro and his brutal regime became known. Some Americans continued to support Cuban Communism but Dickey Chapelle changed her mind about Castro and said she made a mistake to support him. She had covered U.S. Marine combat operations during World War II and in Korea. In August 1965, she visited 2nd Battalion, 9th Marines in Vietnam and stopped briefly to speak to some members of my platoon while I was serving there as Platoon Commander, Communications Platoon, H&S Company. She said that she had changed her opinion of Fidel Castro along with some other reporters because she knew that he was an enemy of America and the American people. Unfortunately, while covering an operation two months later in Chu Lai, Chapelle accompanied a Marine patrol and was killed when the patrol triggered a booby trap consisting of a grenade and mortar round. In the blast six Marines were also wounded.

First Platoon, Company H, 2nd Battalion, 6ᵗʰ Marines, Camp Lejeune,
May 1962, *author serving as platoon leader center bottom row with
Staff Sergeant Carpenter on the right.*

Many admirers of Fidel Castro in America continued to support him for
nearly five decades regardless of his crimes and hostile actions. No American
president has been able to counter-act Cuban Communism and its evil mini-
empire. Presently, Castro owns a nine hundred million dollar personal fortune
of business and state enterprises. He has devoted his life and all Cuban
resources to do harm to America and has succeeded in part because of the
support of people in New York, San Francisco, Hollywood and in other left-
wing liberal population centers, who sympathize with Communism and help
to propagate wars at home against freedom and justice.

THE HAITI INCIDENT OF 1963

During early 1963, two years before being sent to Vietnam, I was serving
as the executive officer of Company H, 2nd Battalion, 6th Marines and our
battalion was being retrained, reorganized and refitted for duty as the force
in readiness in the Caribbean. On 11 February Battalion Landing Team
2/6 was reactivated for planning, with the sailing date set for the middle of
April. Every unit was readied and thoroughly checked. Meanwhile trouble
was escalating in Haiti as Papa Doc declared himself emperor for life and was
murdering any one who stood in his way. As storm clouds were forming over
Haiti, the 6th Marine Expeditionary Unit was formed under the command

11

of Colonel R. Bross. Our battalion was assigned to the 6th MEU along with the Provisional Marine Air Group 40 which included a helicopter squadron and other air assets.

We loaded out of Morehead City on 22 April 1963 on the USS Boxer, the USS Thetis Bay, the USS Mandan, the USS Hall and USS Loraine County. Company H under the command of Captain Tom Adams was loaded onto the USS Loraine County because we constituted the armored column of the landing force and needed to be able to roll off fast. Our armored column was designed with Port-Au-Prince and Papa Doc in mind because President Kennedy directed that he may want Marines to land there to stop the slaughter of innocent people. The directives from President Kennedy were that he wanted the option to use Marines if everything else fails.

As the executive officer, I supervised the loading of our Amtracs, Tanks and Ontos which would make up the armored column which would play a crucial role if we went into Port-Au-Prince. As things went from bad to worse in Haiti, we had a crisis on our hands with contingency plans being dusted off. Then President Kennedy declared an emergency and our task force rushed to the coast of Haiti where we remained in international waters to wait for further orders.

We were aboard ship for over a month. As during the Cuban crisis we read all available reports and wanted to know what Papa Doc was doing to cause trouble. After a week of waiting at sea, Colonel Robert Heinl arrived from Washington to brief our task force and he came to our ship. He had been a naval attaché in Haiti for a long time until he was ordered out of the country by Papa Doc.

Colonel Heinl told us that Haiti was the poorest country in the hemisphere and suffering under a ruthless dictatorship based on the predominance of black people over any other race. The darkest skinned people were the rulers in the highest positions and made up the dreaded Tontons Macutes secret police which terrorized the people of Haiti. Lighter skinned people were relegated to subservient roles. The flag of Haiti consisted of the French tricolor with the white part in the middle torn out.

The Tontons Macutes were recognizable by the white suits and dark glasses they wore, according to Colonel Heinl, with handguns under jackets. They sometimes executed people on the spot. Many political prisoners were taken to the Bastille in Port-Au-Prince where they were tortured and killed. Children were seen playing soccer outside the large prison with the heads of decapitated inmates.

Most of the ammunition in the country was stored in the basement of the presidential palace. The palace had been blown up several times in the past during uprisings by the people. The only telephones and utilities which worked had been installed by Marines during the American occupation of the country from 1916 to 1934. Marines ran the country and created a lawful society with a working economy out of banditry and anarchy. Under Papa Doc the country slipped back to chaos and mass slaughter of innocent people causing an uproar in the world and a crisis in Washington.

While diplomats were negotiating with Papa Doc our ships were on the horizon to let him know that we could land any time to arrest him and restore order. Members of the news media arrived to cover the crisis and were billeted on the USS Boxer. Our battalion had a Royal Marine exchange officer, Captain Leslie Hudson, who after serving as an assistant operations officer was given command of company E. During the days of waiting at sea, company E performed not only our close order drill but also that of the British Royal Marines. When the reporters taunted Captain Hudson and asked if he was going to land with us and fight against Papa Doc's forces he said to the reporters that they better not stand in his way.

After our task force was on station in front of Port-Au-Prince for several weeks showing our flag tensions increased. Papa Doc's navy began to try to challenge us in international waters. At first small patrol boats made high speed passes at our ships with guns pointed at us. Then the largest patrol boats which Haiti had made passes at our ship which as a landing ship was sometimes called by our sailors a long slow target. Our captain sounded general quarters sometimes and sailors manned their guns. Finally, we got tired of being harassed and our destroyers appeared. Our destroyers chased the Haitian navy away not to be seen again.

At night we watched the coast and saw camp fires sometimes. Upon closer observation we noted that sometimes voodoo rituals were being performed at the fires. Colonel Heinl told us that if President Kennedy gave the order to land we needed to rapidly secure the presidential palace, the airport and the downtown area where the Bastille was. The best way to capture the palace and Papa Doc was with our armored vehicles. We studied street maps and were given directions by Colonel Heinl. Our armored vehicles were to be led by Captain Adams in a command tractor up front and I as the executive officer was to bring up the rear with an alternate command group. If the lead vehicles were blocked or held up, Captain Adams could ask me to take over as the front of the column and keep it moving to capture the palace.

As in Cuba, after our ships were on station ready for action any moment, and we waited and waited for the order to go, there was a diplomatic solution to the crisis. Papa Doc was given a deal and a golden parachute which eventually landed him in exile in France. Marines were never landed but a victory was achieved for the people of Haiti and the free world.

CHAPTER 2 –
FOURTH ESTATE OR FIFTH
COLUMN

COMMUNIST AGGRESSION IN 1965

During early 1965, President Lyndon Baines Johnson had to deal with Communist attacks in Vienam and in the Dominican Republic. Fidel Castro wanted to create another Cuba in the Dominican Republic and President Johnson said he did not want another Communist takeover and enslavement of a country in Latin America sponsored by the Soviet Union. In Vietnam, Communist forces infiltrated the Republic of Vietnam with the support of the People's Republic of China and the Soviet Union and were threatening Da Nang and Saigon.

The Main Stream Media (MSM) or Fourth Estate in America, along with the left-wing of the Democratic Party with its interest groups, were largely supporting the romantic story of Castro and Che Guevarra in Latin America and the revolutionary history of Ho Chi Minh in the fight for Communism in Vietnam. In the Dominican Republic, President Rafael Leonidas Trujillo was painted as the bad person by American reporters since he was a right-wing dictator and not like Castro. In Vietnam, the news media painted Ho Chi Minh largely as a sainted firgure and not as a Communist mass murderer and thug which he was, in my opinion.

Thanks to editors of the New York Times, the Los Angeles Times, the Washington Post and other liberal news organizations, along with politicians and interest groups of the Democratic Party, actions taken by President Johnson to counter Communist state sponsored terror and to defend freedom as a part of the Cold War, were increasingly opposed in America. President Johnson was faced with mounting unrest and growing protests because of the hype of the news media and the Democratic Party organizations. The Democratic Party had control of Congress and its platform called for social welfare, aid to third world countries and civil rights.

In April 1965, while serving with the 5th Marines, at Camp Pendelton, California, I remember "Excercise Silver Lance" in preparation for our deployment to the Republic of Vietnam. The news media were not reporting the facts about Vietnam but were opposing President Johnson's plans to send the Marines to help the people of Vietnam against Communist aggression. Although President Johnson was trying to stop mass-murder and enslavement in the Republic of Vietnam, his good deeds were not reported or condoned in the news media. He was vilified and criticized.

5th Marine Regiment Commanding Officer and Staff March 26, 1964,
Colonel Walt Reynolds among commanders bottom row,
second row, author standing third from right, left of Major Franklin C. Broadwell.

On 24 April 1965, President Johnson sent the 6th Marine Expeditionary Unit to the Dominican Republic after notification that a Communist-inspired coup was threatening the government in Santo Domingo and help was requested by President Donald Reid Cabral there. Then the 4th Marine Expeditionary Brigade and a brigade of the 82nd Airborne Division were sent by President Johnson to restore peace and bring back democracy to the Dominican people. However, world Communists and Socialists, Communists in Latin America, at home and in the US Congress, attacked President Johnson for his unannounced and unilateral action. Deep differences between the President and Congress arose in matters of foreign policy. Ideological disagreements continued and were highlighted in liberal newsmedia. Eventually the drum-beats in the news media and Congress against helping the Republic of Vietnam encompassed President Johnson's desire to support democracy in Vietnam against the Communists.

PROBLEMATIC NEWSMEDIA COVERAGE OF THE EVENTS IN VIETNAM

The Geneva Agreeements of 1954 recognized a partitioned Vietnam. It was divided into a northern Communist Democratic Republic in Hanoi led by Ho Chi Minh and a southern free Republic of Vietnam proclaimed on 26 October 1955 in Saigon led by President Ngo Dinh Diem. With the help of Buddhist factions which had been repressed and opposition leaders who wanted more freedom, President Ngo was discredited and overthrown in November 1963 in a military coup, while American diplomats remained neutral. During the political turmoil in Saigon, Communist guerrillas known as the Vietcong occupied several rural areas with the full support of Ho Chi Minh and the Hanoi government. Then the North Vietnamese sent many supplies, infiltrators and Communist cadre to launch a clandestine war against the Republic of Vietnam. Since Ho Chi Minh was supported by Communist China and the Soviet Union, President John F. Kennedy had sent American advisors and special forces to counter the Communists in Vietnam but they were outnumbered and being overrun during early 1965 by the Vietcong and North Vietnamese units sent by the Hanoi government.

In May 1965, after Excercise Silver Lance had been completed at Camp Pendelton, I transferred to Okinawa with 1st Bn, 5th Marines. Then I landed in Vietnam on 6 July 1965, as platoon commander, Communications Platoon, 2nd Bn, 9th Marines operating against Communist forces south of Da Nang, the second largest city in Vietnam which we were sent to protect along with its important airfield and installations. The 9th Marines commanded by Colonel Frank Garretson set up their headquarters on a hill near Route 1 southwest of Da Nang. Our battalion headquarters was collocated at first with the regimental headquarters.

During the Marine amphibious landings on Red Beach near Da Nang, reporters and camera crews were on hand to cover the events. The actions of many members of the news media were hostile and anti-American because they were foreigners who had been hired by media moguls and their news organizations in New York, Los Angeles, Atlanta and San Francisco. Some reporters hired local Vietnamese drivers, typists and secretaries who were eager to help and work for less money because they were Viet Cong infiltrators and Communist agents.

WHO WAS HO CHI MINH?

In general, many reports about Vietnam were factually incorrect, badly researched and heavily slanted in favor of the Communists. Many reporters were influenced by Communist propaganda and admired Ho Chi Minh without knowing who he really was. He was born in 1890 in the village of Kiemlien, central Annam, under the name of Nguyen Tat Thanh. In 1907, he became a primary school teacher and in 1912 he got a job as a ship's steward. During the First World War he worked in the kitchen of the Carlton Hotel in London. In 1918, he moved to Paris and tried to sway the American delegation to the Peace Conference in favor of Vietnam against France. He wrote articles for socialist publications and was a founding member of the French Communist Party.

Officers of 2nd Battalion, 9th Marines, 3rd Marine Division, Okinawa,
June 1965, *bottom row Capt. R. Lawrence, Capt. C. Dean, Maj. Jack Buck, LtCol.*
G. Scharnberg, Maj. Joe McClernon, Capt. R. Lloyd Jr.,, Capt. L. Osborne,
Second row from bottom, author third from left.
On author's left, Capt. J Guggino and Capt. P. Gormley.

From 1922 to 1925, Ho Chi Minh was in Moscow were he was trained as a Bolshevik revolutionary and subsequently accompanied the first Soviet advisors to China. In 1930, he moved to Hong Kong where in 1931 he was arrested for sedition. The French colonial authorities already regarded Ho Chi Minh as a dangerous revolutionary and asked the British to hand him over to them but the British refused. In 1940 he tried to stage an uprising in

Hanoi and Saigon but had to flee to China where with the help of Chinese Communists he established among exiles the Viet Minh movement. On the orders of Chiang Kai-shek, he was kept in prison from 1941 to 1942 but was released in 1943 to return to Vietnam to organize Communists against Japan. He declared a Democratic Republic of Vietnam on 2 September 1945 after the Japanese were defeated and turned his recruited Viet Minh to fight the French.

The Viet Minh fought from 1946 until 1954 against the French colonial government in Vietnam with massive military aid by Mao Tse-tung and Joseph Stalin, culminating in the victory of General Giap at Dien Bien Phu. After the Geneva Agreement of 1954 tacitly recognized the presidency of Ho Chi Minh in north Vietnam, he claimed authority over the whole state and supported the Viet Cong insurgency in south Vietnam from 1963 onwards. Many American reporters had been conditioned by Communist and left-wing social democratic propaganda to sympathize with the Viet Minh against the French and with the Viet Cong against America.

THE ZIPPO LIGHTER INCIDENT

An example of biased and incorrect reporting became known as the "Zippo Lighter Incident" among Marines and others serving in Vietnam. News media editors hyped fire exchanges with Viet Cong into an atrocity by Marines against the civilians in the village of Cam Ne. Previously, on 9 July 1965, after our unloading had been completed on Red Beach, we established a perimeter near Route 1 and the Vu Gia river. The next day we received incoming mortar fire from across the river from the Viet Cong but could not return fire because permission was delayed between MACV (Military Assistance Command Vietnam) and civilian authority.

Since we then received sniper fire and occasional mortar fire from across the river, our battalion established a Forward CP near the Route 1 bridge. On 11 July, elements of our reconnaissance battalion and Company B, 1st Battalion, 9th Marines, were sent across the river by Colonel Garretson. After a few hours, the advancing Marines came under a large volume of fire from several directions. The Viet Cong were entrenched in fortified tunnels dug sometimes under the homes of civilians and under storage facilities. When fire was returned some huts were damaged in several villages.

After the fire exchanges continued for several days and became significant, reporters and camera crews arrived from Saigon. Then a few weeks later, at the village of Cam Ne, Moreley Safer who was a Canadian citizen and known for his liberal leftist views, perpetrated the "Zippo Lighter Incident" with his camera crew. A Marine private was asked to pose with a Zippo lighter in front of a straw hut to show how he would burn it down to destroy an enemy tunnel entrance. The Marine tried to please the reporters fearing no evil intent and posed for the photograph which was hyped by Safer and his editors into an atrocity against the civilian population. The media moguls embelished and hyped the photograph into a sensational story back home that we were burning the homes of innocent civilians and Safer won fame and later the Pulitzer Prize. That photograph set the tone for the whole war. It was taken out of context to shock the American people. The news media did a disservice which was perpetuated many times over and over again during the Vietnam war.

While the Viet Cong and North Vietnamese Army (NVA) could not defeat us on the battlefield, the political officers in Hanoi launched a campaign in America to turn public opinion against the war. News media moguls such as Catherine Graham who owned the Washington Post, left-wing politicians who controlled Congress and well known liberal reporters of the New York Times and Boston Globe, along with television anchors like Walter Cronkite and Dan Rather wore out and defeated the American public handing victory to the Communists.

No matter what was done right during many operations and battles with the Communists to keep the Republic of Vietnam free from its invaders, it did not make the news. News was made by taking any photo, like the one of a Zippo lighter being used to burn a straw hut, embelishing it so that it would shock the American public and turn it against the American Armed Forces and President Lyndon Johnson. Photographs for television were selected out of context to shock the American people so hard that when the pictures were shown on the evening news at dinner time, the whole family would choke on their food and would not be able to eat it.

At first we did not get our mail while operating against the Viet Cong. When the mail did arrive we found out from family and friends that the Zippo lighter photo which had been hyped into an atrocity by editors back home made the front page of Life magazine and caused a Congressional investigation eagerly conducted by left-wing Democrats in the U.S. Congress about why we were committing atrocities against the population. Lieutenant Colonel George Scharnberg, the commanding officer of 2nd Battalion, 9th Marines and Lieutenant Colonel Verle Ludwig, the commanding officer of 1st Battalion, 9th Marines were angry and frustrated. Many years later they told me that the injustices created by the news media and the Pulitzer Prize committee in New York were vicious anti-American lies and someone in addition to God should punish these evil perpetrators.

The newsmedia moguls, televison anchors and editors were making huge profits and salaries from stories which denigrated our victories and disrespected the patriotic young men who showed the greatest love for their country by giving their lives in combat and paying for freedom with their blood. The news media owners and writers were often distorting the war to make money by inciting class, gender and racial warfare at home and supporting the Communists overseas instead of reporting the facts and serving the American people.

JOURNALISTS AND THE FIFTH COLUMN

In March 1970, after returning from Vietnam I thought we were winning the war against Communism after the North Vietnamese Army had been defeated in the South. What I did not know was that the war was being fought on several fronts. While we were winning on the ground in Vietnam we were losing the television, news paper and propaganda war. The Communists had a proven system and chain of command of political officers, developed first in the Soviet Union, which fought with propaganda, television and newspapers backed up by secret police and money.

While the North Vietnamese could not defeat us on the battlefield, they decided that they could win the war on American and European television, in newspapers around the world and in political parties. Ho Chi Minh, as one of the founders of the French Communist Party knew how to play the propaganda game. He and other Communists planted information backed by lots of international money against America.

It was a shock to me to hear what journalists and reporters were saying about Vietnam. It was also a shock to find out that the television anchors like Walter Cronkite enjoyed enormous influence in America. Reportedly, the Communists started their propaganda war against Vietnam in many countries. Where ever there was a Communist Party with associated left-wing politicians, entertainers, professional feminists, pacifists and haters of America throughout the world, the North Vietnamese with the help of the Soviet Union and People's Republic of China, found fertile ground for their political offensives. They could not defeat the Marines and soldiers in Vietnam but they felt that they could win the war by using the political and social systems in America and the West.

Many American journalists read the abundant Communist and Socialist propaganda and slowly bought into it. The New Year 1968 offensive was a disaster for the Communists by body count ending their ability to conduct guerrilla warfare in the Republic of Vietnam but it was a great victory on television in America. The First Marine Division easily threw back the Communists in Da Nang but that did not make the news. What made the news was that a squad of infiltrators got into the almost empty embassy compound before they were all killed. This fiasco took place while half of all military personnel where celebrating the New Year. Nevertheless, "President" Walter Cronkite declared that the war in Vietnam could not be won and therefore was virtually lost.

A photograph of a Saigon Police Chief executing an infiltrator on the spot for murdering innocent civilians, was used by our media to prove that we were losing the war and were the bad guys. That photograph was played over and over again along with a photograph of a naked little girl running on a hard surface road away from a burning village. The little girl came to America after full recovery and has lived a full life. Our media, nevertheless, without mentioning the circumstances of the photographs, used them to turn our people against our government and in favor of the Communists.

During the Vietnam War, it seems to me, America was a news media oligarchy in which all information was monopolized by three corporate news media businesses, which could care less about Marines and soldiers fighting in Vietnam, because they wanted to make money from advertisements to as many viewers as possible. The three media giants and their editorial staffs controlled all information which was delivered primarily by middle-aged journalist "anchors", like Walter Cronkite at dinner time, to entertain and act out the news for the sale of advertisements.

After the Communists and their fellow travelers fed information to the united press and international news media, through various outlets in many effective ways, it was delivered by the news anchors to the American people. We lost the war it seems, because all the facts in the White House, Pentagon and the Armed Forces were never presented to the American people and were considered irrelevant by many viewers and readers who liked what Walter Cronkite acted out much more than what a President of the United States had to say. The American people then began to hate our Presidents and voted for left-wing politicians who demanded that we give victory to the Communists and not to America during the Cold War. The Americans who were misguided by the Communist propaganda machines and the "anchors" who passed it on, voted to cut and run as soon as possible to abandon the free people in the Republic of Vietnam to the Communists.

In my opinion, the erroneous reporting by main stream media (MSM) and popular anchors like Walter Cronkite, along with later Dan Rather, Peter Jennings, Ted Koppel and Morley Safer among others, turned the American people against the people of Vietnam who were fighting for freedom against Communism as a part of the greater struggle against Communism in the Cold War. By distorting the facts to fit their liberal biases, it seems that some in the news media did great damage to our country and cost the lives of many Marines and soldiers.

The dishonesty and hype of some members of the news, entertainment and education media was exacerbated by the many expensive lawyers they hired to defend themselves when confronted with real facts. The lawyers who were hired had little or no ethics and defended any issue for the right amount of money. When General Westmoreland tried to sue some media moguls after the Vietnam war he had no chance because the media lawyers were the best paid in the field and were bought in advance at any cost.

SCHOOL OF JOURNALISM, PULITZER PRIZE AND ACADEMIA

As a graduate student at Columbia University, I heard comments from journalism students about a liberal bias at our School of Journalism and the Pulitzer Prize Committee associated with the school. The comments were that from the beginning, aspiring journalists were taught a view of the world with a social democratic outlook and the Pulitzer Prize was awarded primarily to reporters for stories which were often anti-American. While I was there, the support for Castro and Communism was strong among the journalism students who would be allowed to graduate and in the journalism faculty.

After decades of anti-American student demonstrations at Columbia University, on 4 October 2006, leftist students of the International Socialist Organization, rioted and stampeded again as they did during the Vietnam War. They threatened and reportedly knocked off the glasses of Jim Gilchrist, a speaker invited by college Republicans, who is the founder of the anti-illegal immigration, border-watching Minuteman Project. As often before, Columbia officials allowed the students to commit random acts of violence and to brake the rules. However, a law suit has been filed against Columbia officials this time and an investigation has been initiated.

Over the years I watched for biases and anti-Americanisms since I could not believe what was often reported to the American people about our wars. There were some examples which had me worried. Morley Safer, according to Lieutenant Colonel George Scharnberg, was awarded the Pulitzer Prize despite the wrong and deceitful Zippo Lighter incident reporting at Cam Ne in Vietnam. Recently, the Pulitzer Prize was apparently awarded for revealing to Islamic terrorists that their finances were being traced by our government and that there were prison camps in Europe. Since his retirement, Walter Cronkite has openly supported liberal causes and expressed dislike for our President and the War on Terror. "Coming out of the closet" as a liberal who claimed to have been unbiased, in my opinion, deserves a more critical look at his past reporting and his grand declaration that the war in Vietnam could not be won.

Similar biases have been widely reported to exist at our universities. During reconnaissance operations in East Germany, against Communist forces from 1971 to 1974, I often observed anti-American propaganda posters on display in many cities with a picture of Angela Davis. She was heralded as a great American activist who was fighting for Communism and violent revolution in America. According to Richard Kirk, of the many Communists teaching today in our schools and universities, Angela Davis is probably the most famous one, having run for Vice-president on the Communist party ticket in 1980 and 1984.

Reportedly, Angela Davis is one of seven such "University Professors" at the University of California and is apparently the only one who gained that title without having produced a serious scholarly work. In about 1970, she fled from the FBI and was tried for taking part in a plot to free her imprisoned Black Panther lover who was awaiting trial for murder. The plot to free her lover resulted in the death of four people, including Judge Harold Haley, whose head was blown off with a sawed-off shotgun owned by Professor Davis. Acting as her own lawyer to avoid cross-examination during the trial, she was found not guilty of the charges against her. She received Communist International praise and propaganda honors from the Soviet Union as a great anti-American revolutionary. She was awarded the International Lenin Peace Prize and given lavish employment by the University of California system.

When I was a student in New York, I was impressed by the high standards in mathematics, science and the arts at the schools. However, I was disappointed by the hotbeds of anti-Americanism dominated by Communist ideology among students and faculty in some schools. The anti-Americanism often manifested itself based on a poor knowledge of history, a lack of understanding of the reality of Communism and no concept or idea of the mass-murders of millions of innocent people by Stalin, Mao Tse-tung, Kim Il Sung, Pol Pot, Ho Chi Minh, Fidel Castro and others.

CHAPTER 3 –
PUSHING THE COMMUNISTS
AWAY FROM DA NANG

A RUMOR OF WAR, AMPHIBIOUS LANDING AND FIRST
TOUR OF DUTY IN VIETNAM

In early June 1965, members of my platoon and the rest of 2nd Battalion, 9th Marines, trained and refurbished our equipment on Okinawa for several weeks. Rumors were flying and we waited for orders. It was surprising to hear that the third battalion of our regiment was already serving in Vietnam where it was deployed by transport aircraft two months before to protect the Da Nang airfield against repeated sapper attacks. Major General Louis Walt, our division commander, then told us that President Johnson was sending the 3rd Marine Division and thereby committing the first regular ground troops to Vietnam to stop the relentless advances by the Communists towards Da Nang and the South China Sea coast where most of the population lived.

In late June 1965, we were formed into a landing team with new attached units and we loaded into ships for an assault landing in Vietnam. We were on the way for several days and then joined a large task force for the landing. The task force commander was apparently not sure about the situation in Da Nang and caused needless delays and waste of time during the landing phase. At 0400 on 6 July, we started to land on Red Beach north of Da Nang without opposition. After the lead companies were ashore, the landing was declared an administrative one and the rest of our battalion with the 9th Marine headquarters behind us landed at their leisure. The first incident took place when a passenger train from Phu Bai struck one of our amtracs driving inland over the rail line. We deployed near Route 1 and the Vu Gia river when sniper fire was received on the beach where our supplies were being unloaded.

It has been said that service to our country is the highest honor and privilege we have as citizens and so the honor and privilege was mine to command the Communications Platoon in Vietnam. Staff Sergeant Heriberto Gonzalez was the Communications Chief, the Radio Chief was Sergeant Edward Peterson, the Comm Center Chief was Staff Sergeant Herbert Wells, and Sergeant Duval was the Wire Chief. Our platoon also had a tactical air control section, an electronics shop and an attached AN/TRAC-27 radio relay section for a total personnel strength of ninety-three Marines. From the moment we landed on Red Beach the demands on us were great because as the first troops in country we covered a large Tactical Area of Responsibility (TAOR) to defend Da Nang which was the second largest city in the Republic of Vietnam.

During the administrative part of the landing our radio vehicles were unloaded late. As soon as possible we used our AN/MRC-38 radio jeep on Red Beach to communicate on the Tactical Net to our new command post about ten kilometers inland. Our battalion had to buy the land for our new command post and in the bartering we had to break down communications there and move many times. As soon as we could, we mounted three radios in Lieutenant Colonel Scharnberg's jeep to keep him in touch with everybody. We gave him an FM, a UHF and a single-sideband radio and assigned our best radio operator to him. We deployed our two AN/MRC-83 radio jeeps and kept the AN/MRC-87 radio jeep ready for use by our two Marine pilots who were our attached forward air controllers.

THE FIRST FIRE EXCHANGES WITH THE VIET CONG

On 9 July our unloading was being completed on Red Beach. The Company H detachment which did most of the unloading joined their company on the battalion perimeter. Artillery battalions 1/12 and 2/12 were ashore finally and then our large freezer was unloaded to keep our batteries out of the hot weather. The freezer kept our dry cell batteries from dying fast and was the idea of Major Howie Henn, the Regimental Communications Officer.Colonel Frank Garretson's 9th Marine staff came ashore and worked to determine the limits of our large TAOR.

Since we were receiving more sniper fire and occasional mortar fire from across the river, our battalion established a Forward Command Post (CP) near the Route 1 bridge. We moved one of our AN/MRC-83 jeeps there for communications with regiment. Our companies were patrolling and setting ambushes at night. Our radios and wire lines were working but our tracked vehicles destroyed some wire lines inadvertendly which had to be replaced. The two forward air controllers were busy day and night and used the AN/MRC-87 a lot.

On 11 July elements of our reconnaissance battalion and Company B, 1/9 were sent across the river by Colonel Garretson. Suddenly Company B under the command of Captain West and reconnaissance Marines under the command of Captain Patty Collins were hit by a large volume of fire from several directions. Our Company G was called in as the reaction force and entered the fire exchanges after an hour. The fire exchanges continued during the day and were considered significant due to the volume and duration of fire. Then Company F commanded by Captain Cliff Rushing was also committed minus one platoon which was providing security on Red Beach. Captain Clyde Dean's Company E was deployed back at the battalion and regimental headquarters for security minus one platoon kept in reserve as a reaction force in case of breakthrough on the perimeter lines.

While I was at the Forward CP supporting operations, Captain Dean was ordered to send a rifle squad to us for security. While I was checking the message traffic which my radio operators were receiving and passing it to Captain Russell Lloyd, Jr., the S-3, Company G reported their second platoon leader (Lieutenant Miller) had been wounded in action (WIA) in the shoulder. A few minutes later Company F reported their second platoon leader (Lieutenant Thompson) also WIA from a gunshot wound in the shoulder. I requested authentication and told Captain Lloyd that enemy snipers were aiming at our rank ensignia which we all polished with Brasso and were shining in the sun. The word was passed then to place the insignia under the collar or smear camouflage cream or shoe polish on them to keep from becoming a target.

The fire exchanges decreased somewhat but continued into the next day. It was decided to send Marines up the river mounted in amtracs and our radio section prepared two command tractors for the operation. Several AN/PRC-10 radios were mounted in each command vehicle and I was in one of them to make sure all worked well when we started up river. The movement was uneventful and the radios worked well. I returned to the Forward CP and the reconnaissance and Company B Marines in the amtracs were withdrawn the next day with no Viet Cong wanting to engage the amtrac column. Instead the Viet Cong fortified the villages along the river and emplaced mines and booby traps everywhere along the way.

SHRAPNEL AT THE FORWARD CP AND MY DIARY ENTRIES

On 13 July 1965, progress was being made in pushing back the Viet Cong from the nearby villages but sporadic sniper and mortar fire was received by companies F and G near the Forward CP. Company H under the command of Captain Paul Gormley returned from a detail in Chu Lai during the day where they had been sent on a priority basis to unload cargo the day before. Company H returned to the perimeter lines and returned sniper and mortar fire when two of my radio operators and I received minor shrapnel wounds at the bank of the Song Vu Gia river.

The two radio operators were evacuated by helicopter with a civilian man who had been hit by a Viet Cong mortar round in a nearby village and needed immediate attention. I sat along side of Route 1 holding a bandage to the right side of my neck when Major Vincente Blaz our regimental S-3 drove by and asked how I was. I said I was fine but in reality I could not stop the bleeding from a small piece of shrapnel which had lodged itself in my neck. My uniform was soaked in blood when a driver arrived with an ambulance and drove me to Company C, 3rd Medical Battalion.

The medical battalion was not set up yet and only had a few tents up with cots in them. I was given a Tetanus shot and the bleeding was stopped. I was told that the shrapnel in my neck would not be removed and to this day it is still in my neck. My uniform was washed during the night and I rested on one of the cots. The next day I was told that I was lucky that the piece of shrapnel did not go further into my vital organs and that I would be returned to duty in a few days. I would be given permission to go, I was told, when doctors felt I was strong enough. I fell asleep on one of the cots and when I woke up, I decided not to wait for the written permission. I got dressed, walked to a nearby road and caught a ride back to the Forward CP. The Purple Heart was awarded to me many years later in Arlington, Virginia.

At the Forward CP, companies F and G conducted operations to remove the snipers and enemy mortar fire. Marines used the amtracs again to patrol up river while others probed along an abandoned rail line berm leading to Hill 55. Since fire was received from Duong Son1 it was surrounded but then snipers opened up from outside of the village to add to the confusion. Lieutenant Colonel Scharnberg then sent Company E across the river where fire was received by them from Duong Son2, Cam Ne2 and Phong Le1. Company E lost Lieutenant Bush in action and had a total of nine Wounded in Action (WIA).

On 16 July, our security platoon was attacked on Red Beach and Corporal Bell was killed in action (KIA) after our tanks left to come to our forward perimeter. It was proposed to move our battalion command post across the river to Duong Son1 and I considered setting up a TRC-27 radio relay back to regiment. Then Sergeant Duval said he could lay wire lines along the abandoned rail line and over the Route 1 bridge and I agreed. Our battalion was getting ready to push forward and to expand our perimeter.

On 17 July we established liaison with the US Army advisor and Republic of Vietnam Army (ARVN) training camp in our TAOR. We gave them a flame throwing tank demonstration and established direct communications by laying wire to them and putting their line into our battalion switchboard. The ARVN troops conducted patrols, practiced assaults with blanks and live ammunition in their training area which was on our right flank. It was a wonder that no one got killed by the Marines or ARVN up to that point.

On 18 July we found a suspected wiretap into our wire lines by the VC. Our wire section laid about 40 miles of lines which had to be maintained and policed. Some Marines were ill due to lack of sufficient salt and salt pills were handed out as temperatures reached 115 degrees during the day and up. We had trouble policing our wire lines due to the work load and we could hardly keep up with laying the lines to our fast moving rifle companies. Our radio communications, however, worked well.

On 19 July it was decided not to move our battalion CP forward yet. It was intended to move it to the school house just North of Quang Chan2 and it would have been a suitable area for the CP. Our wire lines were cut in several places. Some housewives cut sections of wire from our lines to use as clothes lines for their laundry. Sergeant Duval began a program to overhead our lines on homemade bamboo telephone poles which worked well for us. I passed the word to destroy all used batteries before being discarded to keep the VC from using them in electrically detonated box mines and booby traps.

We found the village of Doung Son1 to be filled with man holes with punji stakes in them, all kinds of punji stake traps and tunnels under houses. In the center of the village a house was painted by the ARVN with slogans in the day and by the VC at night. Reporters came to Duong Son1 to investigate how we burned down a hut with flares during the night which we fired sometimes from our perimeter to light up the area in front of our lines. I guess they were disappointed that the hut was burned by accident and they could not accuse us of another atrocity but I am sure they tried. There was no development in Vietnam that the news media did not treat as a setback for us and television back home was jaw-droppingly defeatist and one sided while young Marines were risking their lives.

On 21 July our tanks were deployed to protect the battalion CP and the forward outpost (OP). Tanks used their search lights at night sometimes to check the rice paddies for any movement. Our amtracs patrolled the river. A platoon of company F relieved the company E security detail at our Forward CP at the Song Cau Do railroad bridge. Two tanks and two amtracs were attached to the company F platoon for support. Our Tactical Net was loaded down with users and I asked to keep the administrative traffic on other radio nets. Staff Sergeant Williams who did a superb job leading our electronics repair section got transfer orders to another unit. He was the first among many in an inter-battalion exchange of people to make sure that when our tour ended not everybody went home at the same time.

JOINT OPERATIONS WITH ARVN AND
POPULAR FORCES

On 23 July the Marines of company H commanded by Captain Paul Gormley were returning sniper fire when ARVN soldiers also fired at the VC snipers from nearby. In the exchanges of fire 1 ARVN soldier was killed and 1 was wounded by our friendly fire. We requested that an ARVN liaison officer be assigned to our forward CP and I gave him one of our AN/PRC-10 radios. Then a joint sweep was conducted by Company H and an ARVN platoon of the Phong Le1 area. Company E under Captain Clyde Dean held Duong Son1. The third platoon of company H swept through Phong Le1 and then established a perimeter line. When the ARVN platoon was asked to go through the village they said they could not be ready until noon so we asked the local Popular Forces unit to go with us and they were ready and moved out.

On top of Marble Mountain, Da Nang, Vietnam, July 1965.

Our battalion was then ordered to conduct a reconnaissance in force operation South of Marble Mountain and along the coast. Lieutenant Colonel Scharnberg accompanied by Colonel Garretson, moved to the area with two companies and conducted the operation with 2 VC KIA and about 10 enemy weapons captured. We wanted to be in contact with our main CP during the operation and I set up a TRC-27 radio relay antenna on the top of Marble Mountain. In order to get the antenna mounted we had to climb the mountain and that took about two hours. When we were approaching the mountain top we found to our amazement a Buddhist monastery and temple inside the middle of the mountain. There were VC tunnels also in the mountain. During the night we had fire exchanges with the VC. The monks were completely hidden inside the mountain and so they were surprised to see our radio relay section moving smartly through the monastery. The antenna worked well when there was no wind. Sometimes there was a strong wind on top of the mountain and we had some static. During the first night, Captain Lloyd received a personal message which was passed to Lieutenant Colonel Scharnberg who took it to Colonel Garretson to let him know that he had been selected for promotion to Brigadier General.

All our AN/PRC-10 and AN/PRC-6 radios were being used. My records showed that I utilized 70 miles of wire in about two weeks. Our battalion operations tent was finally strong-backed with lumber which we received from Red Beach. We built wooden floors for other tents and got ourselves and our equipment above the wet and soggy ground. We tied our communications in with the ARVN by both wire and radio. Our companies moved every day and radios worked well. Our wiremen were fired on by VC several times while laying and overheading lines.

The tempo of operations continued non-stop and we began to experience a shortage of personnel to maintain all the wire lines and radio nets. Major Milton Irons became the new regimental communications officer and he was against using the TRC-27 much. The TPS-21 system was employed and we needed more TPS-21s. On 24 July Companies E and H were expanding our area of control with an ARVN unit deployed on our left flank. Company H conducted sweeps through Quang Chan1 and held Phong Le1. During the night ten rounds were fired over my tent by the VC.

Some of our vehicles near the Cau Do River, Vietnam, 1965.

MOVING SOUTH ACROSS THE CAU DO RIVER

During the last days of July we maintained our Forward CP near the Phong Le Bridge and directed more operations across the Cau Do River to push the VC south and away from Da Nang. Company E swept through Duong Son1 and set up a perimeter from which they patrolled. One patrol came face to face with a VC unit when they met on a trail but the Marine on the point fired faster resulting with 1 VC KIA and several VC WIA. Company H under Captain Paul Gormley with First Lieutenant John Belcher as the XO worked out of a perimeter immediately south of the Phong Le Bridge with an ARVN platoon attached to them.

Company H moved through Quang Chan1 and then held Phong Le1. We lost radio contact with them during the night of 25 July when they ran out of batteries but the wire lines worked. The next day our Air Liaison Officer (ALO) First Lieutenant William (Billy) Baldwin obtained Tactical Air Direction (TAD) frequencies for our tactical air control radio operators for easier talking to F-4 Phantom close air support aircraft and helicopters. We joked that we could tell bachelor pilots who flew low from married pilots who dropped their ordnance when flying high because they wanted to come back home to their wives.

On 26 July the District Chief provided an additional platoon of troops to sweep Cam Nam and to hold a part of Route 1. On 27 July we experienced a battery shortage due to heavy use of radios and we closed down our TAC net except for emergency use or wire line failure. A program was started to rotate platoons from the perimeter lines back to our battalion rear area for a few hours so that Marines could clean up, get a hot meal and get new gear if needed. On 28 July Company H was sent to Chu Lai to help with the perimeter of a newly established enclave. I decided to send Staff Sergeant Gonzalez, Corporal Eyler and Lance Corporal Brewin with a PRC-47 single side-band radio with Company H for long range communication with us. Company H took with them 3 AN/PRC-10s, 6 AN/PRC-6s, phones and wire and all equipment worked well.

On 29 July we were able to establish radio communications with Company H in Chu Lai and we maintained contact. In the morning one of the radio operators in my platoon drove me across the Phong Le Bridge across the river and I visited companies E and F to get first hand information about communications. I began a practice of taking a radio jeep which had been operating all night and was carboned up for a ride to make staff visits and to get the carbon out. Our Tactical Net was working well with everybody and I counted that I had 35 AN/PRC-10 radios committed in the battalion with 3 in repair at Force Logistics Support Group and 2 being repaired in our platoon. We also had 28 AN/PRC-6 platoon level radios committed along with 139 EE-8 field telephones.

The next day the BA 279 batteries which we requested on an emergency basis arrived but our wire supply was still critical. It was raining all day making it harder to communicate and keep the equipment dry. Our Naval Gunfire Liaison officer arrived without communications equipment and we had to assign a radio operator to him with our equipment. The artillery forward observers (FO) from 12th Marines came with their own radios on artillery frequencies and provided redundancy and backup for us. If our radios were to go down it was always good to know that we could call the artillery for a relay of messages.

On 31 July a sweep was conducted by Company F through our TAOR to the boundary with 1/9. At the end of the sweep Captain Rushing reported Lance Corporal Medlin as missing. Captain Lloyd at that point asked Lieutenant Baldwin for a helicopter for a search for the Marine. When the H-37 arrived mounting 2 M-60 machine guns, I jumped in with Captain Lloyd, Lieutenants Baldwin and Raske (the executive officer of company F) and we flew low over the rice paddies where Captain Rushing's company had been operating and the missing Marine was last seen. As we searched the area, Captain Lloyd had the helicopter sit down several times in different hamlets where the missing Marine's patrol had been. In each one, we would run out with weapons drawn and search the huts in the area for the missing Marine. The fourth time we did so, we received small arms and semi-automatic weapons fire from an estimated platoon of VC on the other side of a rice paddy. We raced back to the waiting helicopter across fifty yards of paddy dikes and scrambled aboard the aircraft. As Captain Lloyd boarded and the helicopter lifted off, it was hit several times by enemy fire. The crew chiefs made good use of their M-60 machine guns and we departed the area safely. As we did so, Lieutenant Raske sustained a foot wound. We deposited him at the nearest unit of the 3rd Medical Battalion and returned to the 2/9 Forward Command Post. Then Lieutenant Colonel Scharnberg, moved with a company of Marines mounted in LVTs to the area which we had just left and recovered the Marine who had fallen asleep in high grass surrounding a hamlet.

SWEEPS IN CONJUNCTION WITH OPERATION BLAST OUT I

On 1 August a six-man patrol from Company H was hit resulting in 1 KIA and 2 WIA. An extensive air support operation was initiated with A-4 and F-4 aircraft against the VC/NVA but enemy casualties were unknown because casualties if any were dragged away. A number of 500lbs bombs were used and communications worked well. We requested a change of our Table of Equipment (T/E) to add an SB-86 switchboard to our inventory and one more URC-22 switchboard. A sergeant TPS-21 technician was assigned to us and I sent a letter requesting the new AN/PRC-25 radio for our battalion as soon as possible.

Intelligence revealed that the VC were maintaining a roadblock near the railroad tracks between Duong Son2 and 3 manned by a four-man unit. About 40 VC lived in Duong Son1 and 2 setting in booby traps, punji traps and built underground bunkers. Enemy political officers were active and VC tax agents collected 270 piastres annually from each family. The attitude of the villagers was generally friendly to the VC and unfriendly to the ARVN. Company B, 1/9 commanded by Captain West swept through the area again and were fired on by the VC. The company uncovered 267 punji traps, 6 Malayan whips (a bamboo tree bent backwards), 3 grenade booby traps, 6 anti-personnel mines and 1 multiple booby-trapped hedgerow. The troops demolished 51 huts and 38 tunnels. VC fire was returned with 105mm artillery and 81mm mortars.

Companies E and H swept the area while company G was held as our battalion reserve. Company F was deployed south of the Phong Le Bridge. Additional intelligence information placed elements of the 18th NVA Regiment in our area. Sappers from the regiment had attacked the Da Nang airfield just before we arrived in Vietnam and withdrew through the area covered by our TAOR. Company H engaged a VC unit resulting in 3 VC KIA and 2 VC captured.

During the first day in Duong Son1 Company B, 1/9 lost 3 Marines KIA and 4 WIA. A patrol from Company A, 3rd Reconnaissance Battalion was attacked in the same area by about 100 VC/NVA resulting in a radio operator WIA and First Lieutenant Frank Reasoner KIA. Reasoner ignored the heavy volume of fire and moved to the side of the wounded Marine, killed 2 VC and silenced an automatic weapon. Despite this, the VC wounded the radioman again before he reached cover. Again ignoring the intense enemy fire, Reasoner moved to the Marine's aid but was mortally wounded himself. He was awarded the Medal of Honor.

On 6 August the ARVN I Corps commander Lieutenant General Thi and General Westmoreland removed restrictions on Marine operations south of Da Nang. Determined to keep the pressure on the VC, Lieutenant Colonel Scharnberg intensified our patrols and sweeps. Almost daily, company sweeps moved through villages and rice paddies. At 0300 on 11 August, Companies G and H jumped off on a sweep while Company F was holding the railroad track. A fire exchange in Duong Son2 resulted in 20 VC KIA with Second Lieutenant Richard Regan killed in action and 14 Marine WIA.

Author with AN/MRC–83 radio jeep, Duong Son, Vietnam, 1965.

During the sweeps we kept four radio nets up and operating. One of our Ontos tracked vehicles got stuck in a rice paddy and needed a recovery vehicle. Captian Joe Guggino was allowed to use a house in a village for his

Company G command post which reduced his exposure to sniper fire. Wire lines to Companies G and H were cut by the VC during the night. Sergeant Duval and our wire section worked during the night to repair wire lines and captured four VC.

Our companies used 292 antennas when holding up for improved radio transmissions. Company H moved out and forgot their 292 antenna in one of the villages. I drove with one of our radio jeeps to the junction of Route 1 and 1A to look for places for wire lines and antennas. Helicopters chopped up our overhead lines by the bridge. We were using PO2 poles to overhead the lines since villagers complained when we cut poles from bamboo trees which were private property. We made every effort to be of assistance to the villagers and to respect their needs.

CHAPTER 4 –
THE FOG OF WAR AT HOME AND
A DIFFERENT STORY IN VIETNAM

ELIMINATING THE 1ST VC REGIMENT DURING OPERATION STARLITE

It was reported that President Johnson watched the television news often in his office during the Vietnam war. However, the news media were not reporting the facts and were living in a fantasy land presenting lots of anti-Americanisms. After President Johnson sent the 3rd Marine Division to the northern part of the Republic of Vietnam, many successful operations were conducted by the Marines. Our regiment, the 9th Marines, conducted operations to push the Viet Cong away from the Da Nang area and kept a battalion at the airfield for security.

After the Army of Vietnam (ARVN) I Corps commander Lieutenant General Thi and General Westmoreland removed restrictions on Marine operations south of Da Nang, some encouraging news came to President Johnson two weeks later. On 20 August, upon urgent request to us from Chu Lai to borrow our radios and telephones for Operation Starlite, my communications platoon sent AN/PRC-47 and AN/PRC-10 radios and many of our telephones by helicopter to the 4th Marines and the 7th Marines who had surrounded the 1st Viet Cong (VC) Regiment.

During Operation War Bonnet, Vietnam, 1965.

We were told that a Marine re-supply column of amtracs with rations and water had blundered into the headquarters of the 1st VC Regiment and the Marines in the column were fighting for their lives. Four Marine battalions surrounded the area and killed 614 VC by body count, took nine prisoners and 42 suspects, captured 109 enemy weapons at a cost of 45 Marine KIA (Killed in Action) and 203 WIA (Wounded in Action). Additional VC hiding in the area were killed or captured during the mop up after the battle.

On 11 September, our battalion conducted a sweep of Hill 55 with two companies and a "Flying CP" consisting of the Battalion CO, S-3, ALO and CommO with radio operators and wire men. As the CommO and Communications Platoon Commander, it was my duty to provide the radios and wire along with personnel to operate the equipment. Our battalion commander was often called on to fly out or force march with the light command group and two or three companies to County Fair pacification, Golden Fleece rice harvest protection or other operations.

During the next nine months, I kept my light marching pack, my weapon, two hand grenades and two LAAWs (Light Anti Armor Weapon) always ready to go on short notice. Lieutenant Colonel Willian Dohahue, our battaliion commander, would get a phone call at any time (day or night) from our regimental commander and sometimes we would be moving out in an hour or two by helicopter, by vehicle or on foot. Often our command group would go out with two companies for a few days and come back to the CP only to change radio operators and the two companies for rested Marines who could operate around the clock. We participated in many large operations, continueously conducted small unit patrols, many night and day ambushes and cordons. By the end of the month, we had cleared one-third of the way to Hoi An and covered nine villages south of the Cau Do river.

GUARDING THE DA NANG AIRFIELD

Then out turn came to provide airfield security to the Da Nang airfield and relieve 3rd Battalion, 9th Marines who had guarded the airfield for about six weeks. We began to coordinate our replacement of 3/9 from our TAOR and found that there was a lack of unity of command at the airfield. Defense was divided between tactical perimeter and patrol duties which we were assuming and internal security. The air base commander was Lieutenant Colonel Hung, CO of the Vietnamese Air Force (VNAF) 41st Tactical Wing and he had overall defense responsibility. A Marine Colonel was named Base Defense Coordinator under whom our battalion assumed tactical duties while the many tenant units were each charged with their own internal security. A joint communications center was established and we were given two huts there to set up communications to our many higher and subordinate commands.

During October as the Air Base Defense battalion our assignment was less dangerous but in some ways more wearisome and demanding than combing the rice paddies for VC south of the Cau Do river. On the night of 27 October, a VC/NVA raiding force apparently came by boat to our air facility north of Marble Mountain used by Marine helicopters of MAG-16. Under cover of mortar fire which engaged Seabees nearby at least four sapper teams attacked the helicopter field and nearby hospital in the rear of 1/9. Marines killed 41 VC/NVA but 6 sappers with demolitions got unto the helicopter parking mat where they destroyed 24 helicopters and damaged 23. Three Americans were KIA and 91 WIA but most wounds were minor.

The same night, sappers attacked Chu Lai airfield also resulting in 15 VC/NVA KIA but 2 A-4 aircraft were destroyed and 4 damaged. Our battalion was on full alert at the airfield and we called in artillery on all likely approaches towards Da Nang during the night. When morning came, evidence was found that a VC battalion attack against Da Nang itself had been averted. Numerous blood trails in an area 18 kilometers west of Da Nang indicated that the VC had been hit hard and dispersed. About the same time, 10 kilometers south of us, a 3/9 squad ambushed a VC company moving towards the airfield killing 15 VC while many more WIA were dragged away by the retreating VC.

The monsoon came on in force in October and by November the rain was averaging an inch a day. Logistics problems increased as roads turned into mud and storage areas were damaged. High waves made the unloading of supply ships difficult and the build up of Da Nang and Chu Lai slowed down as engineers and Seabees had to conduct repairs. We started to plan our departure from the airfield during the end of October and our return to our tactical area south of the Cau Do river. Although we had made a lot of progress, there were reports that Ho Chi Minh was sending NVA units to our area to save the VC from total annihilation and there were reports that the NVA 325A division was operating south of us and that the 1st VC Regiment had been reconstituted.

While we were preparing to return to our tactical area, we found out from our division G-3 that many operations were planned for us. The VC maintained five battalions in our area and conducted both small scale harassments and large scale attacks. They announced a hate the U.S. month and we assumed greater alertness for that time. Demonstrators appeared in front of our installations and we searched for explosives after the demonstrations. A VC night attack against 1/1 nearby resulted in 46 VC KIA and 10 VC captured with relatively few Marine casualties.

OPERATIONS GOLDEN HARVEST AND HARVEST MOON

During early December our battalion participated in Operation Golden Harvest to protect the rice harvesters by conducting many patrols, ambushes and cordons. Seismic Intrusion Detectors (SIDs), Claymore mines and new AN/PRC-25 radios issued for fire support requests and coordination were of great help to us. VC casualties were increasing while our relatively low casualties were being reduced even more in our operations. It was difficult to get exact enemy body counts since the VC tied communications wire around their wrists and used meat hooks to drag away their many WIAs and KIAs.

Then Operation Harvest Moon was planned after the VC moved eastward into the Phuoc Valley threatening the garrisons at Viet An and Que Son. The 1st VC Regiment reinforced by elements of the NVA 325A Division became active after the ARVN withdrew from Hiep Duc in late November. Control headquarters was Task Force Delta under Brigadier General Jonas Platt, who was my former regimental commander when I served with the 6th Marines. The ARVN forces from the 2d ARVN Division were commanded by General Lam.

Our battalion participation in Operation Harvest Moon consisted of sending Companies E and G to 3/3 and Company H commanded by Captain Paul Gormley to 2/7 commanded by Lieutenant Colonel Leon Utter. The ARVN made contact with the enemy on 8 December and after heavy fighting Marine battalions 3/3 and 2/7 entered the battle. On 10 December, 2/1 which was the Special Landing Force entered by helicopter against heavy resistance. Between 12 and 14 December four B-52 strikes were made in support of the Marines for the first time in the war.

During Operation Double Eagle, Vietnam, 1966.

Radio operators of our battalion were able to listen to Task Force Delta tactical nets and it appeared that by 16 December, VC/NVA resistance had faded, allowing 3/3 to start marching out of the valley to the northeast. Then 2/7 followed in trace and on 18 December ran into an attempted ambush at Ky Phu, west of Tam Ky, when our attached Company H was hit while bringing up the rear of Utter's battalion. The VC/NVA got the worst of it with 105 KIA but Captain Paul Gormley and one of my attached radio operators were KIA along with several Marine WIA. PFC Lucas was attached from my platoon to Captain Gormley to operate an AN/PRC-41 UHF radio for communications with aircraft and was in the company command group when Captain Gormley was hit in the legs by a 57mm anti-tank round. But PFC Lucas was ok because his radio on his back stopped a bullet fired at him. First Lieutenant Harvey Barnum, the attached Artillery Forward Observer, called in fire support against the ambush exposing himself to enemy fire repeatedly and was awarded the Medal of Honor. PFC Lucas was awarded the Bronze Star.

During the operation, our 2/9 command group and the rest of our battalion in the rear, while receiving sniper fire to keep us busy, was ordered on 15 December to move south by truck convoy to relieve 3/3. As we were about to go, we were told to stand down because the VC/NVA were filtrating out of the operation area and clearly on the run. The operation ended with 407 VC/NVA KIA, 13 crew-served and 95 individual weapons captured along with a large amount of enemy supplies found on the reverse slope of the ridge south of Que Son.

ARMORED COLUMN DURING OPERATION WAR BONNET

Upon standing down from having to relieve 3/3 in Operation Harvest Moon, we started to plan Operation War Bonnet which was a five company armored column down the beach south of Marble Mountain. Under the command of Lieutenant Colonel Donahue we assembled one comapny of tanks, one company of Ontos, one company of amtracs, our command group to include our new S-3 Major Angelo, First Lieutenant Baldwin our ALO and me with our Companies E and H, Company B of 1/9, Company L of 3/9 and Company K of 3/3. The VC scattered in all directions as the armored column worked well and drove almost to Chu Lai before returning, resulting in 1 VC KIA and 50 VC captured. We mounted our radios in two command amtracs. A platoon of LVTH amtracs with mounted 105mm howitzers as the main armament was used for the first time in our area.

Upon return from Operation War Bonnet, we noted on our calendar that it was 4 January 1966 and we had entered a new year. As 1965 ended, there were 180,000 U.S. troops in country and 38,000 were Marines. Major General Walt visited us and told us that we had done well. Brigadier General English also paid us a visit and said that with two-thirds of the 1st Marine Division in place, Major General Lewis Fields would move his flag forward to Chu Lai. The zone of action assigned to the First Marine Division coincided with that of the 2d ARVN Division in Quang Tin and Quang Ngai provinces which were in the souther part of I Corps. The 5th Marines were scheduled to arrive in June.

After an attack by the VC against 1/1 on our right flank, which was repulsed with 50 VC KIA and about 100 WIA, Operation Long Lance was conducted by 1/1 and our battalion blocked in support of the sweep which resulted in 18 VC KIA, 10 VC captured and 39 VCS (VC suspects) detained. On 11 January, our Company G was sent by our battalion to participate in Operation Mallet after several days of planning and preparation. In addition, on 15 January we participated with our whole battalion in Operation Big Lodge which ended on the 19th with a four day truce at the time of the lunar year "Tet" as it is known in Vietnam. On 25 January, after using the truce to set up, the VC launched an 82mm and 120mm mortar attack against Da Nang and the Marble Mountain air facilities causing 2 American and 2 Vietnamese KIA and a number of WIA.

SEARCHING FOR THE 325A NVA DIVISION DURING OPERATION DOUBLE EAGLE

After Tet, our battalion was attached to Task Force Delta for Operation Double Eagle against the NVA 325A Division believed to be in the Quang Ngai and Binh Dinh provinces. The operation started on 28 January 1966, with 3/1, 2/4 and 2/3 conducting the largest amphibious operation of the war so far in our area, where the NVA 325A Division was engaged the previous November. On 31 January, our battalion was helolifted to ready positions at the Quang Ngai airstrip and the next day we marched into the mountains northwest of the coast to exploit B-52 strikes conducted on suspected NVA positions.

During Operation Double Eagle, President Johnson arranged a visit for the Washington Post columnist Joe Allsop to our battalion as a VIP (Very Important Person) to observe the war directly from the front lines. President Johnson was hoping that the columnist would write something positive about our fight for freedom against communism. The columnist and his escort officer arrived by helicopter despite dense fog and poor visibility. The helicopter landed near my foxhole and Mister Allsop spent about 30 minutes with us observing everything and asking questions.

President Johnson was concerned that the news media were not accurately coverning the war at home and wanted reporters and columnists to see for themselves that the Republic of Vietnam had been invaded by communists who were mass murdering the population and perpetrating many atrocieties. The problem even early in war was, that just as in the "Zippo lighter incident", our mainstream news media back home were selling news papers and television shows, by fabricating bad news and horror stories about our allies and our Armed Forces, while giving the communitsts from North Vietnam the benefit of the doubt and a pass for all the many murders, acts of terror and criminality against the people of the Republic of Vietnam.

On 19 February 1966, our battalion was flown out of the area back to our rear, with 312 NVA/VC KIA and phase one of the operation completed. Then we heard that some elements of the NVA 325A Division were concentrating west of Tam Ky and north of Chu Lai. Phase two of Operation Double Eagle was initiated by Task Force Delta and our battalion conducted Operation Rough Rider during which we moved south on Route 1 in an armed convoy to Tam Ky and the new battle area. There we fought with the NVA until 1 March, resulting in an additional 125 enemy KIA by body count.

MAN-EATING TIGERS, SOVIET AND CHINESE ADVISORS

Upon return to our battalion rear Marines were debriefed about the operation. Some repeated the observation that they saw several tall Caucasian advisors with the VC who may have been Soviets. Other observations of tall Chinese advisors were also reported which could not be pinned down and fully confirmed. The report that man-eating Tigers were stalking the battlefield to eat dead bodies was confirmed when a Marine shot a Tiger with his .45 caliber pistol and the dead Tiger was found to be huge. The Marine was on an outpost when the Tiger dragged him out of his foxhole. Saved by his helmet and body armor the Marine was able to draw his pistol and fire while being dragged by the Tiger. When the incident was first reported by radio the Marine was verbally reprimanded and disbelieved. After he showed them the dead Tiger then everybody shut up.

Upon our return we heard that Major General Wood B. Kyle took command of the 3rd Marine Division and wanted to eliminate the VC south of Da Nang including the Doc Lap Battalion operating north of An Hoa. A series of operations followed which involved our regiment and sometimes our battalion. Operation Kings expanded our TAOR to Route 14. Operation Georgia deployed 3/9 to the southwest and our battalion participated in sweeps for several days. Operation Liberty broadened the front of our enclave by bringing the 3rd Marines on our regiment's right flank and the 1st Marines on our left. On the Da Nang air base, the 1st Military Police Battalion relieved 3/3 and freed the battalion for duty with the 3rd Marines.

At the same time, northwest of Phu Bay Operation New York was started when the 810th Main Force VC Battalion attacked the 1st Battalion, 3d ARVN Regiment and 2/1 conducted a night helicopter assault in support of the ARVN resulting in 122 VC KIA, 6 crew-served and 63 individual weapons captured. On 3 March, Operation Utah was conducted when elements of the 2d ARVN Division engaged the 36th NVA Regiment in the vicinity of Chau Nhai village and Marine helicopters flew in 2/7 and the ARVN 1st Airborne Battalion followed by 3/1, an ARVN battalion and 2/4. Under the command of Lieutenant Colonel P.X. Kelley, 2/4 landed to the south and closed the last opening in the ring around the NVA regiment. In one landing zone an F-4 Phantom aircraft was shot down by the NVA. With elements of 1/7 and ARVN scouts sent to block southwest of Binh Son, by dawn of 6 March Marines had 358 NVA KIA and the ARVN had 228 NVA KIA.

On 9 March, according to General Simmons, the Special Forces camp at A Shau garrisoned by 17 Green Berets and 400 Vietnamese was attacked by about three NVA battalions. The fight lasted for two days during which three Marine UH-34s and one A-4C aircraft were lost while 12 Green Berets and 172 Vietnamese were lifted out successfully. On 19 March Operation Texas was conducted after the reconstituted 1st VC Regiment attacked a Regional Force company in an outpost northwest of Quang Ngai. On 20 March 3/7 and the 5th ARVN Airborne Battalion landed near the outpost while 2/4 blocked seven kilometers to the south resulting in 405 VC KIA after four days of fighting. On 28 March in Operation Indiana in the same area 1/7 landed behind elements of the 1st VC Regiment who were attacking the 3d Battalion, 5th ARVN Regiment resulting in 69 VC KIA and 19 weapons captured.

CHAPTER 5 –
CIVIL UNREST IN VIETNAM

DEMONSTRATIONS IN SAIGON, DA NANG AND HUE

In addition to some hard fighting against the VC/NVA, between early March and late June there was civil unrest in the Republic of Vietnam. On 10 March, according to Brigadier General Edwin H. Simmons, Director of Marine Corps History, our flamboyant I Corps commander General Thi was reprimanded and relieved of duties by Premier Ky's National Leadership Committee. Gen Thi was a member of the committee along with nine generals who voted to oust him for insubordination. Soon pro-Thi antigovernment demonstrations started in Saigon, Da Nang and Hue.

On 13 March, many shops closed down in Da Nang in protest, students went on strike and some workers stayed at home. The leaders of the civil unrest formed the Military and Civilian Struggle Committee and on 15 March they called for a general strike. On 1 April, Lieutenant General Pham Chieu was detained by Buddhist students in Hue as a demonstration that the Saigon government no longer ruled in I Corps. On 4 April, 3,000 members of the 1st ARVN Division marched in Hue behind their division band demanding the overthrow of Premier Ky and the Saigon government.

Premier Ky announced in Saigon that he would use loyal troops against the demonstrators and three battalions of the elite Vietnamese Marines were airlifted to Da Nang. The U.S. Marine advisors excused themselves and came over to our regiment where we asked them what was going on. The exact position of ARVN troops in I Corps was not clear. It seemed that the 1st ARVN Division was in the Buddhist camp against the government while the 51st Regiment and the Ranger battalions were divided. The 2d ARVN Division was relatively quiet while troops in Hoi An were strongly in support of the struggle forces.

Our battalion was ordered to make plans for the evacuation of civilians from Da Nang. On 9 April, our command group with one company left ongoing operations against VC in our TAOR for a while as we drove all the way back to Da Nang in a Rough Rider type convoy of trucks with machine guns mounted. After we arrived we provided protection for the helicopter evacuation of 750 American noncombatants, which took place rapidly and without incident. Our command group then rushed back to our TAOR as a mechanized column of anti-government ARVN troops left Hoi An on Route 1 towards Da Nang. Our Company F cut the column in half by contriving a truck breakdown on the Cao Do Bridge. The lead vehicles, which proceeded towards Da Nang, were then fired upon and set on fire by the Vietnamese Marines resulting in a withdrawal by the anti-government troops. After it was all quiet the Vietnamese Marines returned to Saigon.

OBSERVING THE PRO-THI 51ST ARVN REGIMENT

During the civil unrest period, one of our AN/MRC-83 radio jeeps was carboned up from running day and night in the CP and needed to be taken out and driven. The driver and I took the vehicle out on Route 1 and as we picked up speed heading south we saw the entire 51st ARVN Regiment halted on the opposite side of the road on the way to Da Nang. The lead vehicles came into view just as we picked up speed to get the carbon out of the engine and I decided to keep going to avoid a confrontation. As we passed in review I counted over 300 vehicles. At the end of the column we turned around and passed the entire regiment again hoping that they would not fire at us since they obviously had turned against the government, which we supported.

Since they did not fire at us we drove rapidly to our CP and reported what we saw. I was told that the regiment had abandoned its fort and its ammunition supply to the VC and was halted only because Major General Paul Fontana, the Commander of the 1st Marine Aircraft Wing, said that he would blow them away if they kept moving. Major General Walt also intervened trying to broker a deal with the rebel troops. After several days the 51st ARVN Regiment returned to its positions but the harm had been already done. The VC had resupplied themselves with the abandoned ammunition and began using many more mines and booby-traps against us immediately.

MY DISAGREEMENT WITH AN ELECTRICALLY DETONATED 40-POUND BOX MINE

As the Battalion Engineer Officer I wanted to exchange our old 5KW generator for a new one at the maintenance float of FLSG in Da Nang for a long time. The request for replacement was always denied for insufficient justification and we kept patching up the generator until it died one morning. We hooked it up to a truck and I followed in an AN/MRC-83 jeep with the radio operator as driver as we started towards Da Nang on a dirt road not far from our CP. The VC had planted an electrically wired 40-pound box mine in the road and decided to detonate it to get the generator instead of the truck or our radio jeep. As I looked up, it seemed that I saw our generator in the sky before I heard the explosion. We ran towards the tree line with our weapons drawn along the electrical wire used to detonate the mine but the VC were gone. The three Marines on the truck were not injured. I took pieces of the generator in our jeep to FLSG and told the hard-nosed sergeant that this time we had a good justification for a new generator and he finally agreed.

The civil unrest caused some damage to the pacification program. The VC wanted to destroy the Ngu Hanh Son program which was started after the Honolulu Conference between President Johnson and Premier Ky at which expanded civic reforms in combination with military action were approved. The VC interrupted the work of rural construction and efforts to build democracy during the unrest until May. The VC reinfiltrated the hamlet cadres and launched terrorist attacks during the unrest. Two companies of VC were intercepted by 1/9 five kilometers south of An Track a civic action showplace and wiped out before they could do more damage. To help repair the damage 3/1 was brought up from Chu Lai into a five-village area and moved in side by side with the badly shaken 59th Regional Force Battalion. The combined patrolling soon greatly improved the security of the area and the VC were pushed out and defeated again.

Platoon Commander, Communication Platoon,
2nd Batallion, 9th Marines
Vietnam, 1966.

END OF THE CIVIL UNREST AND THE 324B DIVISION
CROSSES THE DMZ

It was a relief to me to learn that the civil unrest was ending. The last centers of civil unrest and Buddhist resistance in Da Nang were the three principal pagodas. On 23 May the pagodas were taken and resistance ended in our area. The 51st ARVN Regiment returned to helping us in our operations and pacification efforts. Until the uprising, the 51st ARVN Regiment under the command of LtCol Lap provided security and led in rural reconstruction work in our area. Their efforts were resumed at the end of May and the VC were pushed back out.

The Buddhist resistance lasted longer in Hue where American noncombatants were evacuated for a second time before rioters burned down the U.S. Consulate on 31 May. Premier Ky then sent government troops into Hue and they had the city under control on 19 June. Three days later Vietnamese Marines and paratroopers took over Quang Tri city and brought civil unrest in I Corps to an end.

It seemed to me that the civil unrest made I Corps more vulnerable. The Soviet trained Ho Chi Minh and his Central Committee in Hanoi apparently saw that too. They decided that the time was favorable to send the 324B NVA Division across the DMZ while the Buddhists infiltrated by the VC were rioting. According to General Simmons, Marine reconnaissance units and 2/1 were sent into northern Quang Tri province to counter the advance of the NVA and Operation Hastings was initiated. The airstrip at Dong Ha, about 50 kilometers north of Hue, was used to bring in 2/4 and 3/4. Contact was made near Cam Lo on Route 9 and 3/5, 1/1 and 1/3 entered the fighting along with five Vietnamese battalions. For the first time B-52 strikes were conducted in the DMZ. The operation ended with 824 NVA KIA and 214 weapons captured. The NVA of the 324B division were well trained and well equipped with Chinese made weapons of Soviet design.

After the NVA withdrew back across the DMZ, three Marine battalions remained to guard against reentry. Soon the NVA came back with fresh troops and Operation Prairie was launched resulting in 943 NVA KIA after several months of fighting. The operation then continued through the rest of the year until 31 January 1967 involving seven Marine and three ARVN battalions, and 1,397 total NVA KIA. In a related operation, Deck House IV, the 1st Battalion, 26th Marines (1/26) came ashore north of Dong Ha as the Special Landing Force (SLF) resulting in 254 NVA KIA. The 5th Marine Division had been activated in Camp Pendleton on 1 March 1966 and 1/26 was the first element of the famous World War II division to reach Vietnam.

OBSERVATIONS AT THE END OF MY FIRST TOUR OF DUTY IN VIETNAM

With the return of the 51st ARVN Regiment into blocking positions south of our TAOR and their help with County Fair operations our battalion had a number of successful contacts with the VC. One of the best company size operations was conducted by Company E under the command of Captain Robert Driver which resulted in 119 VC KIA and 80 weapons captured. Our patrols and ambushes also scored successes. As my first tour of duty ended in Vietnam a growing list of military victories and more political stability was encouraging to President Johnson who said that he believed there was a light at the end of tunnel. Marine operations helped to provide the light as the VC and NVA fled in every engagement.

During my tour with 2/9 we contributed to many battalion and regimental size operations. We conducted numerous patrols, ambushes and small unit actions. Captain Clyde Dean and others complimented me that in all kinds of weather and terrain we never lost communications with our units. Fire support, medical evacuation and operational traffic always worked in our battalion. I served under three regimental commanders, two battalion commanders, three executive and two operations officers before I left. Our platoon performed in an outstanding manner at all times.

A recommendation for the Bronze Star was submitted in my behalf by Lieutenant Colonel William F. Donahue and Lieutenant Colonel George R. Scharnberg for meritorious service in connection with operations against insurgent communist (Viet Cong) and North Vietnamese regular forces. It was stated in the citation that I displayed technical and military proficiency as the platoon commander, communications platoon of 2/9, supervised communications support for our battalion and attached units from arrival in combat throughout diverse commitments and operations, exhibited sound knowledge of infantry communications needs and repeatedly exposed myself to hostile fire in the execution of my duties. It was added, that I accomplished all assigned tasks under often trying conditions through the diligent application of personal leadership principles. Although the recommendation was downgraded later to a Navy Commendation Medal with the combat "V" distinguishing device, I was grateful to both battalion commanders under whom I served in combat for the award recommendation.

After all the accomplishments Premiere Ky awarded the Vietnam Cross of Gallantry Unit Citation and President Johnson awarded the Presidental Unit Citation to our division. The citation stated that we who served in the 3rd Marine Division demonstated extraordinary heroism and outstanding performance of duty in action against the North Vietnamese Army and Viet

Cong forces in the Republic of Vietnam from 8 March 1965 to 15 September 1967. Throughout this period, our division operating in the five northernmost provinces of the Republic of Vietnam, successfully executed its three-fold mission of occupying and defending terrain, seeking out and destroying the enemy, and conducting an intensive pacification program. Operating in an area bordered by over 200 miles of South China Sea coastline, the mountainous Laotian border and the Demilitarized Zone, our division successfully executed eighty major combat operations, carrying the battle to the enemy, destroying his forces, capturing thousands of tons of weapons and material.

In addition to these major operations, more than 125,000 offensive counterguerrilla actions, ranging from squad patrols and ambushes to company-sized search and destroy operations, were conducted in both the coastal rice lands and the mountainous jungle inland by our division. These bitterly contested actions routed the enemy from his well-entrenched positions, denied him access to his source of food, restricted his movement, and removed his influence from the populated areas. In numerous operations, our division worked with and supported units of the Army of the Republic of Vietnam.

In July 1966, our division moved to the north to counter major elements of the North Vietnamese Army moving across the Demilitarized Zone into the Quang Tri Province and fought a series of savage battles against the enemy, repeatedly distinguishing itself and forcing the enemy to retreat across the Demilitarized Zone. Imbued with an unrelenting combat spirit and undeterred by heavy hostile artillery and mortar fire, difficult terrain, incessant heat and monsoon rains, our division, employing courageous ground, heliborne and amphibious assaults, complemented by air, artillery and naval gunfire support, inflicted great losses on the enemy and denied him the political and military victory he sought to achieve at any cost. The courage and aggressive fighting spirit of our division in battle after battle against a well-equipped and well-trained enemy, often numerically superior in strength, and the great humanitarian aid to the peoples of the Republic of Vietnam, reflected great credit upon the Marine Corps.

Major General W. K. Jones presenting the Navy Commendation Medal with
Combat "V" Distinguishing Device, Navy Annex, January 1967.

In I Corps, according to General Simmons, the III MAF directed the
build up of nearly 60,000 Marines while I was there with a total of 7,300
enemy KIA as a result of operations and 4,000 enemy KIA as a result of small
unit actions. In 1966, Ambassador Henry Cabot Lodge said that we had
beaten the NVA and the main force VC battalions. The remaining challenge
was to deal with reinforcements from Hanoi, Bejing and Moscow, along
with about 150,000 terrorist guerrillas who looked like civilians and were
highly organized throughout the country. In late 1965, the Marine Corps was
authorized an additional 55,000 spaces and was building toward a strength of
278,184 by 1 July 1967. By comparison, in Korea Marine strength peaked at
261,343 and during World War II the all-time high strength of 485,113 was
reached. In 1966, the Marines took in 80,000 volunteers and 19,000 draftees
to support the war in Vietnam.

AT THE PERSONNEL DEPARTMENT BEFORE
RETURNING TO VIETNAM

After my first tour of duty in Vietnam, I served for over two years as a
Section Head, Personnel Department, in the Navy Annex of the Pentagon.

The casualties in Vietnam were all reported to us and we processed the required paper work. We were kept abreast of combat operations and the progress being made in Vietnam. Shortly after I departed 2/9, it was sad to read one morning in the message traffic that Corporal Leland "Skipper" Albury of Key West, Florida, who was a member of my platoon was killed by a land mine. His friends and family in Key West established a monument in his honor at the downtown city park where he used to play as a young boy. When visiting Key West, I always stop by at the park to pay my respects.

In Vietnam, according to General Simmons elections were held in late 1966 to choose members of the Constituent Assembly who drafted a new constitution. No one expected a large turnout but 80.8 percent of the people voted despite VC terrorism on election day that resulted in 19 voters killed and 120 wounded. Buddhist threats to boycott the election failed as in Hue, stronghold of the Buddhists, a surprising 84 percent of the registered voters cast their ballots. President Johnson was uplifted by the results and efforts were made to protect the population better through proven Marine pacification programs and combined actions that had worked against the VC.

During 1967 there were four successful elections in Vietnam. In April elections were held for village officials and in I Corps the voter turnout was 82.3 percent. In May, 78.8 percent of registered voters participated in hamlet elections. In September, presidential elections were held in accordance with the new constitution. Despite an intense VC campaign involving 272 acts of violence in which 672 civilians were killed or kidnapped in I Corps, 86 percent of voters cast their ballots. The election named Nguyen Van Thieu as president and Nguyen Cao Ky as vice president. A fourth election in October was held to fill the government's lower house and in I Corps voter participation was 77.9 percent.

As 1967 ended there was reason for optimism. The communists made the northern provinces of I Corps Tactical Zone the main battle area but were defeated each time they attempted to go on the offensive. The III MAF was given U.S. Army troops and the Korean Marine Brigade to reinforce the 3rd and 1st Marine Divisions against increasing NVA forces in I Corps. Pacification programs regained momentum after the Buddhist uprisings ended and the NVA attacks across the DMZ were repulsed. The Republic of Vietnam had shown the world despite of continued misreporting by U.S. media that it could elect a democratic government.

During 1967, Marines conducted 110 major operations during which the communists were defeated and over 356,000 small unit operations with a total of 17,876 enemy KIA. Marine air flew 63,000 sorties in direct support of Marines and 10,000 sorties in support of Free World Forces. Marine air also flew 11,000 strike missions over North Vietnam. Marine helicopter units flew 490,000 sorties during the year. Marine losses were 3,452 KIA and 25,994 WIA in 1967 compared to 17,876 enemy KIA and over 100,000 enemy wounded. From the wounded Marines who required hospitalization about 85 percent were returned to duty.

As 1967 was coming to an end, additional attacks by fire took place against III MAF bases. Dong Ha was hit by three separate attacks totaling 150 rocket and artillery rounds resulting in one Marine KIA and 17 slightly wounded. Then 24 probable 140-mm rockets hit the Marble Mountain air facility causing 5 Marine KIA and 84 WIA. Phu Bai was hit by 50 mortar rounds badly damaging 4 helicopters and lightly damaging 14 more with 3 Marine KIA and 54 WIA. The Da Nang airbase and FLSG were hit by 140mm and 122mm rockets with three Air Force transports heavily damaged and 9 airmen wounded. The launch sites for the attacks were fired upon rapidly by artillery and casualties were minimized by swift reaction.

MCNAMARA'S WALL ALONG THE NORTHERN BORDER OF THE REPUBLIC OF VIETNAM

On 7 September, according to General Simmons, Defense Secretary McNamara announced his decision to have a barrier constructed along the northern border of the Republic of Vietnam which became known as "McNamara's Wall" or "McNamara's Folly". The project was opposed by the Marine Commandant and other Marines who served in Vietnam. One corporal said, the NVA will simply walk around it or in some places step over it. Another Marine said it would take the whole Marine Corps and half the Army to guard the wall. Others said that we sent the best and the brightest to fight and left the dumbest and most cowardly back home to run the war.

While serving in the Personnel Department, we were told that significant personnel and equipment changes took place during 1967 also. Lieutenant General Walt who had led III MAF for two years was replaced by Lieutenant General Robert E. Cushman. Major General Donn J. Robertson took command of the 1st Marine Division from Major General Herman Nickerson who became deputy commander III MAF. The CH-46 helicopter replaced the UH-34 in Vietnam greatly improving Marine helicopter operations. The M-16 rifle replaced the M-14 in Marine units and at first there were problems with the introduction of the new rifle. Then modifications were made and with improved quality control the problems were resolved.

We were told at Headquarters, US Marine Corps, that one of the most successful Marine programs in 1967 was the combined action platoon in which a Marine rifle squad joined a Popular Force platoon to provide security for a hamlet or village. At the end of the year there were 79 combined action platoons organized into 14 combined action companies in I Corps. As 1967 ended, 59 villages were being protected and combined action platoons conducted about 4,000 ambushes and patrols per month resulting in a total of 456 VC/NVA KIA and 256 VC/NVA captured during the year.

We read in classified situation reports in the Personnel Department that at the beginning of 1968 despite of many successes all was not bright. A major NVA invasion was being prepared by Hanoi across the DMZ and the 36-hour truce for Tet celebrations was marred by 16 major enemy violations. At the same time, the Soviet Union and the People's Republic of China sent thousands of weapons and many supplies to the communists to support their attacks against the Republic of Vietnam. The Kalashnikov automatic rifle AK-47 and the follow on AKM was delivered in large quantities to the VC as the currency of socialist solidarity free of charge. Many 122mm rockets along with artillery and mortars were also delivered.

Classified situation reports, which I read daily in Washington, DC, stated that in mid-January, the 304th NVA Division crossed the border from Laos and joined the 325C Division outside Khe Sanh. The 308th NVA, the 325C NVA and the 341st NVA Divisions crossed the DMZ into I Corps as part of a Hanoi coordinated nation-wide offensive started during Tet celebrations. Most of the ARVN troops were on holiday leave and the communists knew that most soldiers were at home with their families when on 30 January Hanoi launched its offensive. The main efforts in I Corps were directed against Da Nang which was attacked by the previously deployed 2d NVA Division and Hue which was attacked by at least eight VC/NVA battalions and the 6th NVA Regiment.

During early February, Khe Sanh had been relatively quiet since the fighting in April and May of the previous year but Marines of 1/26, 3/26 and 1/9 along with one ARVN Ranger Battalion were told to dig in because four NVA regiments were preparing to attack. On 6 February, the 66th NVA Regiment, 304th Division, accompanied by units with flame throwers and nine Russian made PT-76 tanks overran the Lang Vei Special Forces camp six miles southwest of the base. Marine helicopters rescued 14 soldiers and 85 Montagnard fighters and flew them to Khe Sanh. Air strikes and artillery took a heavy toll of the NVA destroying three PT-76 tanks. A NVA battalion attack against Company A, 1/9 was repulsed from the base perimenter. The base was subjected to heavy shelling but ground contact became more sporadic and limited after the NVA took heavy losses from air and artillery.

It seemed based on classified reports that it was prudent when General Westmoreland, expecting NVA attacks across the DMZ, ordered the 1st Air Cavalry Division and the 101st Airmoborne Division to I Corps under the operational control of the III Marine Amphibious Force commanded by

Lieutenant General Robert E. Cushman. The III MAF's TAOR remained the same covering all of I Corps with its northern five provinces of the Republic of Vietnam. The U.S. Army 23rd Infantry Division (Americal) and the Korean 3rd Marine Brigade were assigned to the III MAF in the southern part of I Corps. There were U.S. Navy Seabee units and Navy support personnel with III MAF along with about 7,000 Airmen at the Da Nang air base. Also, the Republic of Vietnam had nearly 81,000 ARVN troops in I Corps under the command of Lieutenant General Hoang Xuan Lam.

CHAPTER 6 –
OBSERVATIONS DURING
SECOND TOUR OF DUTY IN
VIETNAM

REQUESTING ORDERS TO RETURN TO VIETNAM

During my second year at the Personnel Department, with the reports of an enemy offensive in the making, I requested orders to return to Vietnam for a second tour of duty. While I waited for orders, according to General Simmons, by the middle of February of 1968 the Tet offensive had been defeated and the enemy was through. Hanoi had not gained the support of the people as expected in communist propaganda and the news media. American forces held firm and the ARVN had done surprisingly well with not a single ARVN unit defecting to the enemy. Hanoi had won no battlefield victories or gained new territory but instead suffered heavy casualties from Free World Forces. In I Corps, the offensive cost the enemy over 100,000 KIA and about 35,000 weapons captured.

The G-3 Section, 1st Marine Division, Vietnam 1969, *Colonel James Ord standing 6th from right with Colonel Wayne Burt on his right, author bottom row, second from right.*

When I returned to Vietnam in early 1969 for duty, I was given the job of Assistant Combat Operations Center Officer, G-3, 1st Marine Division. The center was located in a bunker on the reverse slope of Hill 327 three kilometers west of Da Nang. The commanding general was Major General Ormond R. Simpson, the G-3 operations officer was Colonel James Ord, the combat operations center officer was Lieutenant Colonel Wayne Burt. My duties consisted of operating the combat operations center (COC) daily from late afternoon throughout the night until morning when I had to give a briefing to General Simpson and the staff about what happened during the night.

In order to comprehend what I was briefing I had to study what took place during 1968 and the Tet 1969 activities. I was informed by old hands that the Tet 1969 offensive which ended just before my arrival for duty was much less than the Tet 1968 attacks. During 1968, with Army reinforcements there were some quarter-million Free World forces in I Corps with 73 infantry battalions. The Marine ground combat strength consisted of 21 battalions from the 1st, 3rd and 5th Marine Divisions. In air strength, there were 14 Marine fixed wing and 13 Marine helicopter squadrons deployed. Personnel figures listed 81,249 Marines serving in Vietnam out of a total of 298,498 on active duty. In comparison, none of the other services had anything approaching this percentage of its servicemen in Vietnam.

During Tet 1968, the year before my return offensive actions started in the Da Nang area in the early morning hours of 30 January with a screen of mortar shells and rockets behind which infiltrated VC/NVA tried to capture the I Corps headquarters. According to General Simmons, the duty section with the help of a Combined Action Platoon blunted the attack until Vietnamese military police and Rangers along with Marine military police finished off the intruders in house to house and street fighting. South and west of Da Nang elements of the 2d NVA Division were intercepted by Marine reconnaissance patrols and engaged by 2/5 and 3/5 after artillery and air inflicted heavy casualties. To the south, in Hoi An, the 51st ARVN Regiment and an ARVN engineer battalion expelled the enemy after heavy fighting. According to General Robertson who sent a congratulatory message to the 1st Marine Division on 10 February, the enemy had not been able to occupy a single objective in the Da Nang area and suffered in excess of 1,100 casualties.

In Hue during Tet 1968, according to General Simmons, the communist infiltrators had an initial advantage because the city was the ancient imperial capital and cultural seat of Vietnam with little security. Security within the city was mostly a police responsibility with no major U.S. installations as at Da Nang. The infiltrators wearing civilian clothes were able to occupy the city before putting on uniforms and launching a surprise attack. During the city's brief occupation, the communists murdered over three thousand innocent civilians which was not reported by news media because it might have been Republic of Vietnam propaganda according to some reporters. During house to house fighting Marines of 1/1, 1/5 and 2/5, along with Vietnamese Marines and ARVN units expelled the infiltrators with NVA remnants being mopped up until 2 March when the battle was declared over.

While the Tet 1968 was not yet resolved, General Westmoreland asked for reinforcements from home and established a MACV Forward command post at Phu Bai on 9 February with General Creighton W. Abrams, Jr., positioned there. The requested reinforcements, the 27th Marines and the 3d Brigade, 82nd Airborne Division arrived into the country. The 27th Marines commanded by Colonel Adolph G. Schwenk along with 2/13, the attached artillery battalion, were given the old but still troublesome sector south of Marble Mountain. The 3d Brigade, 82nd Airborne was attached to the 101st Airborne Division at Phu Bai. By the end of February, there were 52 American infantry battalions operating in I Corps, over half of all infantry battalions in country, 24 U.S. Marine and 28 U.S. Army under the command of III MAF which became the largest combat command held by a Marine with the possible exception of General Roy S. Geiger's brief command of the 10th Army on Okinawa during World War II.

The year before my return saw at first the greatest combat activity of the war in I Corps centered on the two northern most provinces. There III MAF with the ARVN, defeated the NVA which had crossed the DMZ, expelled them from Hue and badly beat them at Khe Sanh. In May, the enemy shifted his attacks against Da Nang and was defeated again as he was also in August. After the August failure, the communists retreated to their bases behind the borders and gave up their efforts to achieve military victory through large-scale attacks. Just before my arrival and during my tour of duty in 1969, the communists reverted to small-unit attacks and harassment with mortar and rocket fire.

SITUATION WHEN I TOOK OVER THE 1ST MARINE DIVISION COMBAT OPERATIONS CENTER NIGHT WATCH

As I began my second tour of duty, the III Marine Amphibious Force, commanded by Lietenant General Robert E. Cushman, Jr., estimated that there were about 90,000 enemy threatening the I Corps Tactical Zone. The enemy order of battle listed 89 enemy battalions of varying strength within I Corps. Along the DMZ, the 3rd Marine Division under the command of Major General Raymond G. Davis was faced with three North Vietnamese

Army (NVA) regiments which were screening the DMZ but avoiding serious engagements. The 3rd Marine Division was under the immediate operational control of the U.S. Army's XXIV Corps which also had the 101st Airborne Division and the 1st Brigade, 5th Mechanized Infantry Division in the northern part of the III MAF tactical area of responsibility.

During my assignment to the combat operations center, the 1st Marine Division under Major General Ormond R. Simpson covered Quang Nam province and generally the center part of I Corps. We guarded the approaches to Da Nang while south of us the 2nd Brigade, Korean Marine Corps, had its own area of operations radiating from Hoi An. Further south, the large Americal Division was operating in Quang Tin and Quang Ngai provinces of the III MAF TAOR. In support of the ground troops, the 1st Marine Aircraft Wing under the command of Major General Charles J. Quilter had fixed wing groups at Da Nang and Chu Lai and helicopter groups at Marble Mountain, Phu Bai and Quang Tri.

The Army of Vietnam's I Corps in which we operated was commanded by Lieutenant General Hoang Xuan Lam. We were there to support his forces and the people of the Republic of Vietnam in their fight against the communists attacking from the north. General Lam's forces consisted of the 1st Division in the north, the 51st Regiment in the center and the 2nd Division in the south of I Corps. The 1st ARVN Division was a crack fighting outfit I was told and comparable to any division in NATO.

On watch in the Combat Operations Center, Vietnam 1969.

During my first day on watch I had to brief the completion of Operations Taylor Common and Bold Mariner. Operation Taylor Common was conducted southwest of Da Nang from December 1968 until March 1969 under the control of the 1st Marine Division's Task Force Yankee commanded by Brigadier General Ross T. Dwyer, Jr. who at the end rotated home and was replaced by Brigadier General Jaskilka. The 5th Marines, 1/3 and 3/3 chopped from the 3rd Marine Division, the 1st ARVN Ranger Group and two Civilian Irregular Defense Groups made up the forces which conducted deep thrusts into enemy base areas using fire support base techniques. Several base areas and a number of caches were destroyed with the heaviest fighting taking place in the "Arizona Territory," a piedmont agricultural area between the Vu Gia and Thu Bon rivers northwest of An Hoa. The operation resulted in 1,398 VC/NVA KIA and 29 prisoners along with 151 Marine KIA and 1,324 Marine WIA.

Operation Bold Mariner started on 13 January 1969 and was conducted by Battalion Landing Teams 2/26 and 3/26 from ships of the 7th Fleet in the three southern provinces of I Corps. Marines came ashore by helicopter and landing craft in the Van Tuong area south of Chu Lai where Operation Starlite had been conducted in 1965. With both Special Landing Force Alpha 2/26 and Bravo 3/26 participating it was the largest Special Landing Force effort of the war. In addition, the American Division moved two battalions into blocking positions from the south to cut off escape routes. The soldiers and Marines then swept toward the sea resulting in 239 VC KIA, about 12,000 civilians screened and 256 VC captured. On 9 February the last Marine units reembarked on the amphibious ships to return to Subic Bay and the operation was over. During 1969, eight more similar landing operations were conducted in I Corps.

At about the same time, the 9th Marines under Colonel Robert H. Barrow conducted Operation Dewey Canyon in the Da Krong valley making skillful use of fire support bases. Three fire support bases were initially built in the jungle and as the regiment advanced other fire support bases were opened in leapfrog fashion. During 18-22 February, the heaviest fighting took place in the center of the advance involving 1/9 and resulted in some of the largest caches of the war being uncovered. At the end of the operation, 1,617 NVA KIA had been counted, 1,461 weapons, hundreds of tons of ammunition, much Soviet equipment and many supplies had been captured.

On 22 February, the 101st Airborne Division began Operation Massachusetts Striker in the A Shau valley to compliment the sweep by the 9th Marines and continued operations into March. On 15 March, the 3rd Marines under Colonel Paul D. LaFond began Operation Main Crag south of Khe Sanh which cost the enemy considerable price in men, weapons and rice by the time it ended on 2 May.

THE TET 1969 OFFENSIVE AND ATTACKS AGAINST DA NANG

The Tet truce in 1969 began on 16 February and again Hanoi used it as a cover for an offensive. However, the attacks were much weaker than the year before due to the previous heavy losses. There were the usual Tet terrorist acts, rocket and mortar strikes, sapper attacks and scattered ground actions. Hanoi's major effort came on 23 February with an attempted large scale move against Da Nang and contained few surprises compared to the previous year. Da Nang was infiltrated, major enemy units came out of the mountains west of the city and a thrust was made from the south through the heavily populated lowlands. The communists attempted to seize the two Route 1 highway bridges over the Cau Do River where I was wounded in July 1965.

Infiltrators north of the river formed one axis of advance while columns from the Cam Ne and Duong Son village areas south of the Cau Do formed the other axis. The 1st Military Police Battalion and 3/1 inflicted heavy losses on the attackers causing them to retreat south. The ARVN and elements of the 1st Marines pursued and harried the withdrawing enemy troops. At about the same time, sappers tried to get to our command bunker and headquarters battalion hoping apparently to disrupt our command and control while NVA regular units moved in from the west. The NVA crossed the valley drained by the Tuy Loan river when they ran into the 7th Marines. A three-day fight ensued during which the NVA were thrown back and lost 289 NVA KIA.

After standing several night watches, I learned the routine and how to handle rocket attacks. After sleeping a few hours during the day, I usually reported to the command center in the late afternoon and read about what happened during the day since I left after giving the morning briefing. Day watches were taken by Major Marty Brandtner and Major Barry Colossard during my nearly eight month tenure. After the day section departed, my section took over. We talked to subordinate and adjacent units on hotlines all night writing down spot and situation reports.

Rocket and mortar attacks against Da Nang usually came after midnight during early morning hours. We usually had tanks on three Observation Posts Eagle, Hawk and Buzzard on hill-tops from which Marines looked into the night for the burning tails of rockets lifting off. When we heard the word "rockets" on the hot line we sprang into action to return fire with tanks and artillery as fast as possible. Village chiefs sometimes did not give permission to fire into their area but we worked things out and got the job done. In the morning, I had to tell General Simpson how long it took us to return fire. I could say most of the time that it was a few seconds because we had pre-registered artillery into likely rocket launch areas and returned fire immediately. Marines were sleeping next to howitzers with lanyards tied to their hands and pulled the lanyards in their sleep when kicked in the leg after the word "rockets" was uttered.

We got so good at returning fire that patrols often found destroyed rockets the next day which never were launched along with blood on trails and other evidence that we hit them after only a few rockets took off. Sometimes out of twenty rockets at a launch site only several were launched and the rest were hit as they were taking off or still in their tubes on mud ramps. Sometimes NVA KIA and weapons were found at the site by patrols the next day.

By plotting the range of 140mm and 122mm rockets on my map it was possible to draw a rocket belt around Da Nang inside which the enemy had to be in order to fire effectively. We sent many day and night patrols into the rocket belt and we harassed and interdicted the enemy by fire. In addition, when rockets were fired observation from any two OPs made it possible to triangulate the launch site and subject it to return fire rapidly. It seemed to me that during 1969 rocket attacks decreased but often lucky hits against aircraft, fuel dumps and personnel were scored causing considerable damage to us.

CAPS, CHU HOIS, KIT CARSON SCOUTS AND STINGRAYS

On 26 March 1969, General Cushman rotated home and turned over a number of successful programs to Lieutenant General Herman Nickerson, Jr., along with command of III MAF. The Combined Action Platoon (CAP) program was highly successful in providing security to rural areas and to assist in pacification. The basis for this program was the combining of outstanding Marine squads with a Popular Force platoon so as to enhance village security. From its beginning in 1965, the program by 1969 had grown into four battalion-size Combined Action Groups, one each at Da Nang, Phu Bai, Quang Tri and Chu Lai. The groups had 19 subordinate Combined Action Companies and these a total of 102 CAPs. In large part due to this and related efforts, we were awarded the Vietnam Civic Action Unit Citation by President Thieu.

The Chu Hoi program consisted of leaflet drops to the enemy promising them safe passage if they surrendered and came over to the side of freedom against communism. During 1969, there were an increasing number of Chu Hois and some of them said that they wanted to fight on our side. The former enemy volunteers were trained by the ARVN and some became Kit Carson scouts with Marine units. They knew the enemy better than any one else and remembered enemy locations which proved to be very helpful during patrols and operations.

The Sting Ray program was another highly successful program operated by the 1st Reconnaissance Battalion under the command of Lieutenant Colonel Drumwright and by other reconnaissance units. It consisted of flying teams deep into enemy territory to hill-tops and other vantage points from which they not only reported enemy movements but sometimes directed devastating blows to enemy units by fire. Sometimes the enemy discovered the teams and an emergency helicopter extract was conducted. LtCol Drumwright participated himself in every emergency extract and did not listen to me and others when we asked him not to do that. Then General Simpson told him that he did not want another battalion commander wounded or killed and ordered him to stay in the rear with the gear. Reportedly Lieutenant Colonel Drumright did not listen even then. Prior to that, during one emergency extract, Lieutenant Colonel Leftwich was in a helicopter which crashed through the jungle canopy and was killed along with the crew.

ARC LIGHTS, GUNFIGHTERS, SPOOKY AND AGENT ORANGE

The STING RAY reconnaissance teams sometimes had to be extracted from areas which would be subjected to B-52 (ARC LIGHT) strikes. We were alerted hours before the strikes but sometimes due to bad weather the B-52s were on their way from Guam while our helicopter squadrons were still trying to extract the Marines. We had some close calls with helicopters flying out while B-52s were almost above them but we never had to invoke a coded request to divert the bombers to secondary targets due to Marines still being in the target area while I was in the command center.

A few times Marine F-4s were overwhelmed with requests for close air support and the U.S. Air Force sent F-4s from its Gunfighter group stationed in Da Nang. When I was told the first time that the Gunfighters would support us I asked if they would fly as low and as accurately as Marines. Then I was educated by my watch section about the outstanding record of the air group leaving no doubt that when the Gunfighters flew the mission would be done right. A number of times when a small Vietnamese unit or a Marine patrol was under heavy enemy fire and needed instant relief the U.S Air Force sent a C-130 "Spooky" with high speed gatling guns mounted in the rear of the aircraft. The Spooky firepower was so great that the earth shook and we used to say that, along with Marine air, artillery and naval gunfire, dignity was added instantly to any common brawl separating the VC/NVA from our troops.

One evening, I had a visit from pilots of an Air Force C-119 squadron in the command center. They asked about enemy firepower in several valleys which they had to spray with Agent Orange. After reviewing the spot reports of previous activity with me they felt that they could do the job without much preparation. Two days later they came back and told me that their aircraft got shot up pretty badly from everybody in the valley. I told them that I heard that when the Agent Orange defoilant was seen coming down, everybody to include enemy, friendly and shades of undecided all fired at the C-119s with any gun they could find. We did not realize that Agent Orange defoliant would cause such a violent reaction.

LIBERTY BRIDGE AND 1ST MARINE DIVISION OPERATIONS

The 1st Marine Division conducted Operation Taylor Common from 7 December to 8 March 1969. Under the control of Task Force Yankee, the operation resulted in 1,398 NVA KIA and 29 NVA POW while Marines had 151 KIA and 1,324 WIA. Operation Lynn River was conducted from 27 January to 7 February 1969, resulting in 58 NVA KIA, 3 NVA POW, 9 Marine KIA and 46 WIA. On 30 March 1969, a new monsoon-proof bridge was completed across the Thu Bon River just south of Dai Loc by the Seabees, completing a direct highway link between Da Nang and An Hoa. The new 825-foot bridge replaced a 60-ton ferry which the 1st Bridge Company had operated since October 1967 after a monsoon flood washed away an earlier bridge.

On 31 March 1969, after the bridge was completed, 7th Marines started Operation Oklahoma Hills. With two battalions of the 51st ARVN Regiment, 7th Marines under Colonel Nichols formed a box perimeter on Charlie Ridge around a suspected base area of the 31st, 141st and 368 NVA Regiments. A fire support base was built at roughly each corner of the quadrangle. Many mines were encountered and after some firefights a regimental-size base camp was destroyed. The operation ended on 29 May 1969 with 596 NVA KIA and 7 NVA POWs while Marines lost 53 KIA and had 482 WIA.

On 27 April 1969, there was a grass fire near an ammo dump two miles southwest of Da Nang which got out of hand. We called them from our command center and offered to bring back a Marine battalion from operations to help put out the fire but we were told that no help was needed from the 1st Marine Division. Soon the fire spread further and then for three days ammunition kept going off until millions of dollars worth of ordinance was gone. A full page photograph of the exploding ammo dump made the front page of the Stars and Stripes newspaper which we posted in our command center with the caption that, "We do not need any help from the 1st Marine Divison" in big letters under the photograph.

On 5 May, Special Landing Force Alpha, made up of BLT 1/26 and HMM-362, conducted Operation Daring Rebel, a cordon and search of Barrier Island with ARVN, Korean Marine and Americal Division units in blocking positions. A number of VC POW and weapons were captured along with large amounts of rice. On 9 May, the 5th Marines under Colonel William J. Zaro intercepted a large NVA force moving from the mountains towards Hill 67 in an area known as the "Arizona territory." Rice and corn markets in that area were plentiful and often used by the enemy. During three days of fighting, the 5th Marines claimed 233 NVA KIA by body count but Colonel Zaro was certain that the enemy casualties were much higher.

On 12-13 May, an enemy force moved towards Da Nang from the south in a corridor formed by Route 1 in the east and the railroad on the west. The 1st Marines, the 51st ARVN Regiment and ARVN Rangers engaged the enemy resulting in 292 VC/NVA KIA. Then on 7 June, the 5th Marines made contact with the newly arrived 90th NVA Regiment in the Arizona Territory. Eleven days of fighting resulted in 320 NVA KIA with the 90th NVA Regiment withdrawing into the hills to regroup. As stated, Operation Oklahoma Hills was conducted by the 1st Marine Division from 31 March to 29 May west of Hoi An resulting in 596 NVA KIA, 7 POW, 53 Marine KIA and 482 Marine WIA. Operation Muskogee Meadow from 7-20 April south of Hoi An resulted in 162 NVA KIA, 16 Marine KIA and 121 Marine WIA.

It was my duty to brief Operation Pipestone Canyon which was directed by the 1st Marine Division on Go Noi Island from 26 May to 7 November 1969. Go Noi Island was a portion of the KY Lam delta between Route 1 and the abandoned railroad and the 36th NVA Regiment was operating from deep underground bunkers there which were hard to find and destroy. Four Marine battalions were used along with two battalions of the 51st ARVN Regiment, the 37th and 39th ARVN Rangers, and a battalion of Korean Marines. A U.S Army engineer company with gigantic Rome plows cleared and plowed the land behind the Marines at the rate of 200 acres a day. In the end, the total was 488 NVA KIA, 28 POW, 54 Marine KIA and 540 WIA.

At mid-summer 1969, my map showed that the 1st Marines were south of Marble Mountain and the 26th Marines were south of Da Nang. Both regiments concentrated on saturation patrolling of the "Rocket Belt" areas that swung around Da Nang at the extreme range of the 140mm and 122mm rockets. The 7th Marines operated from Hill 55 and the 5th Marines worked from their combat base at An Hoa. From 20 July to 13 August, the 5th Marines conducted Operation Durham Peak south of An Hoa which resulted in 76 NVA KIA, 15 Marine KIA and 63 Marine WIA. During this time, 1/7 covered the Arizona Territory while the 5th Marines were gone. On 12 August, two battalions of the reformed 90 NVA Regiment and a battalion of the 368B Rocket Regiment were engaged resulting in 255 NVA KIA, 20 Marine KIA and 100 Marine WIA.

THE BEST SPOT REPORT, LOB BOMBS, ENEMY MORTAR AND ROCKET FIRE

When Operation Durham Peak ended, the 1st Marine Division and Americal Division were shifted southward to give Marines responsibility for most of the Que Son valley, first entered by Marines in 1965 when I was with 2/9. The 7th Marines moved into Que Son valley on 15 August and joined the 196th Light Infantry Brigade in fighting against the 2nd NVA Division outside of Hiep Duc resulting in over 1,000 NVA KIA. Then the best contact resulted at the Thu Bon River when a patrol from Company B, 1/7 observed an NVA battalion starting to cross. The patrol leader reported the sighting and was told to observe and not to fire while the 1st Marine Division prepared a "Time on Target" artillery strike. When the enemy battalion was half way across, combined artillery units supported by the battleship USS New Jersey struck all together with great force resulting in over 450 NVA KIA, over 400 weapons captured, with no Marine KIA and no Marine WIA.

One evening the 5th Marines reported incoming artillery which did not sound right to me because patrols and air observers had not seen any enemy artillery units in the area. Also, the incoming artillery consisted of various caliber shells and pieces of rockets and bombs. Marines said that the incoming shells were slowly flying through the air as if thrown or lobbed by someone and usually exploded as air bursts. Soon Marines called the flying explosives "lob bombs" and upon checking further it was discovered where they came from. It was found that the 368B NVA Rocket Regiment and other NVA units had capable engineers who learned how to fire unexploded ordnance at us from small pits in the ground with jury rigged explosives. Some shells and rockets made in the Soviet Union and China, like some of their weapons, and about ten percent of our shells and bombs malfunctioned on the battlefield. The NVA engineers collected the unexploded weapons and experimented with techniques to fire them at us. Reportedly a number of sappers were killed during tests but eventually they learned how to place explosives in small pits which would launch the ordnance into the air at us with another explosive device attached for detonation. Although Marines sustained few casualties from "lob bombs" they were a topic of conversation and some interest.

Another innovation of the NVA was to send sappers before an attack against us to turn around Claymore Mines so that the mines would fire at us instead of at them. Marines soon caught on to such attempts and covered the Claymores with fire. At the same time, Marine units reported that during patrols, point men who tripped a bobby trap wire learned to get away from the subsequent explosion by running as fast as they could after they felt the wire touch their legs. Many times, Marines on patrols ran out of the bursting radius of a booby trap which took a number of seconds to detonate and were not hurt at all or only slightly wounded. Patrols also watched for water buffalo in the fields and rice paddies. When the water buffalo had been removed from the fields it was a good indication that there was an ambush someplace since the farmers knew where the enemy was and did not want their most prized animals injured or killed.

During nightwatches, I talked to subordinate unit operations officers often and knew precisely what was going on. In the 7th Marines, I sometimes talked to Captian Charles Krulak who was always well informed and could explain what was happening rapidly. After a medical evacuation request was received by the Direct Airsupport Coordination Center next to me and artillery was outgoing at the Fire Support Center near me, I would usually wait a while for spot reports. If none were being sent to me and air or naval gunfire was called along with other activity, I would call and express concern but would ask not to disturb the Marines involved in direct contact with the enemy until an appropriate time was found to report back.

Sometimes spot reports were not needed since we could see what was happening by looking outside the command center. One night, our division headquarters received enemy mortar and rocket fire which resulted in General Simpson's jeep being blown away and the office of Major Charles Robb, in our G-4 Logisitcs section, being destroyed. Since Major Robb was President Johnson's son-in-law, I received many phone calls from III MAF and the White House that night and then Colonel Ord and General Simpson explained that Major Robb was not injured and was not in the office at night when it was destroyed.

THE DAY HO CHI MINH DIED AND A TRUCE WAS DECLARED

On 4 September 1969, Ho Chi Minh died and a three day truce was declared. Ho led the communists with the help of the Soviet Union and the People's Republic of China in all their attacks against the Republic of Vietnam. He was a mass murderer – not on the scale that Stalin was – but he did the best with what he had to kill innocent people who opposed communism. Fidel Castro visited him and the Vietnam communists to show support and solidarity. It was reported that Castro sent Cuban advisors to Vietnam to torture American prisoners and to provide intelligence about U.S. forces. President Carter's former attorney general Ramsey Clark and actress

Jane Fonda also came to Hanoi to demonstrate solidarity along with other far left democrats and socialists. To left leaning radicals, Ho was a sainted figure but to me he was another ruthless communist mass murderer.

On the first day of the truce, it was relatively quiet in the Da Nang area. Many Vietnamese used the truce to visit relatives and families and unfortunately provided cover for enemy movements. On the second day, a NVA commando unit was able to infiltrate through friendly lines to the rear of the 1st Marine Division and attacked our Headquarters Batallion in the late evening. Our headquarters area was guarded by the 1st Marine Division Band which played at County Fairs and ceremonies during the day and manned our perimeter at night. Our band fought a fierce battle with the commandos killing many of them but sustained two Marine KIA.

We heard the fire exchanges in our command center and came out to observe just as an US Air Force "Spooky" aircraft provided air support with a high volume of fire which caused the earth to tremble under our feet. It then seemed that the fighting was over but during the early morning hours more fire exchanges were heard in our area which I briefed to the staff in the morning before going off watch. General Simpson said that we had received some new replacements who probably fired into the morning hours at shadows as green troops are inclined to do.

It did not seem to me to be all friendly fire since I also heard Kalashnikov assault rifles and I asked one of my watch standers to grab his rifle and a jeep. I took extra magazines for my pistol, a couple of hand grenades, and we drove down Hill 327 to see what was going on. As soon as we reached the main road we were in the middle of cross fires between our cooks and the NVA. As we drove further tracers were flying over our jeep. Our cooks were successfully defending their mess hall which had many bullet and rocket propelled grenade holes. We picked up speed and reached our supply storage buildings where clerks, military police and some ARVN soldiers had captured some of the commandos after killing a number of others. Through a translator, I asked the prisoners why they violated the truce. They said that they left the North three weeks ago and never heard about the truce. They had orders to attack our area and did what they had been told to do without any other information.

During September, it was possible to make more staff visits to subordinate units since Marines were starting to redeploy from Vietnam to Okinawa. I visited Hill 55, Hoi An, Cam Ne and Duong Son where I served with 2/9 during my first tour in Vietnam. In Hoi An, it was very sad to hear that West German doctors and nurses who provided medical care to villagers in the area were often killed by the Viet Cong. Eight German nurses who had volunteered to serve the people were brutally murdered by the communists shortly before my visit with of course no mention of it in the news media by the media elite.

It apparently did not matter to anyone that these idealistic young women were unarmed and wore red cross armbands when they were murdered.

During this time, our command center also received many visitors. Our Korean Liaison Officer had visitors from the Korean Marine Brigade who were buying everything they could in the Post Exchange in Da Nang. We also briefed all incoming new officers about 1st Marine Division operations and many others about the forthcoming redeployments. It was very memorable to me to receive an unexpected visit from Tucker Watkins who was serving with the 101st Airborne Division. His father Doctor William Watkins was a famous medical practitioner and surgeon in South Boston, Virginia after serving with the U.S. Army in Burma during World War II. Tucker Watkins later became well known in Virginia politics.

THE THIRD MARINE DIVISION REDEPLOYS TO OKINAWA

During 17 June-16 July 1969, the 3rd Marines conducted Operation Virginia Ridge in the central DMZ area resulting in 193 NVA KIA, 18 Marine KIA and 26 Marine WIA. Then in the vicinity of Con Thien and the Rockpile, the regiment continued engagements with the NVA during Operation Idaho Canyon until 17 September killing 48 NVA while sustaining 25 Marine KIA and 47 WIA. The operation ended on 25 September and it was time to back load on ships for redeployment to Okinawa. The 4th Marines soon followed and also redeployed to Okinawa, leaving the 1st Brigade, 5th U.S. Mechanized Division in Quang Tri province with half of the 1st ARVN Division to guard the DMZ and the Laotian border.

On 16 September, the second increment of the U.S. troop withdrawal was announced. By mid-December, 45,000 Americans would be redeployed and of that total 18,483 would be Marines. The Marines to leave Vietnam were the rest of the 3rd Marine Division, with a proportional share of aviation and service units. The division headquarters, 4th, 9th and 12th Marines returned to Okinawa and the 3rd Marines were sent to Camp Pendleton. During 40 months of combat, the 3rd Marine Division had 28,216 enemy KIA, 499 POW taken and 9,626 weapons captured.

On 7 November, Major General William K. Jones, the Commanding General of the 3rd Marine Division arrived on Okinawa where he also became the Commanding General of the I Marine Expeditionary Force (I MEF). I MEF was the counterpart of III MAF and was established to control Marine ground and air units in the Western Pacific not committed to Vietnam. At the same time, Brigadier General William G. Johnson took command of the newly activated 1st Marine Aircraft Wing (Rear) at Iwakuni and MAG-36, commanded by Colonel Noah C. New, moved from Phu Bai to Futema, Okinawa. Colonel New picked up control of the helicopter sqaudrons, along with VMO-6 and the KC-130s of VMGR-152. MAG-39 was deactivated at Quang Tri and VMA (AW)-533 took its A-6As to Iwakuni from Chu Lai where it joined MAG-15. All helicopter squadrons remaining in Vietnam came under MAG-16 at Marble Mountain with three squadrons operating out of Phu Bai. The responsibility for airfield operation at Dong Ha, Quang Tri and Phu Bai was passed to the Army.

ENEMY ACTIVITY SLOWED DOWN TO TERRORIST AND GUERRILLA CONTACTS

As the III MAF regrouped, combat operations continued at a reduced pace slowing to terrorist and guerrilla acts. Most of the few remaining contacts with NVA units were in the Que Sons and Antenna valley an area held by the 7th Marines. On 7 September, 1/26 and HMM-265 conducted the last Special Landing Force operation of the war in an area south of Hoi An with the 3rd Battalion of the Korean Marine Brigade in blocking positions. The operation resulted in 293 NVA KIA, 121 weapons captured and 2,500 civilians processed. The ceiling on personnel in Vietnam influenced the use of Special Landing Force operations during the next two years. Battalions afloat were kept in strategic reserve for emergencies which did not come about. Since 1965, the 7th Fleet conducted 62 Special Landing Force Operations in Vietnam and of this number 53 operations were in I Corps. The landings resulted in 6,527 enemy KIA, 483 enemy POW and 774 weapons captured.

In late October 1969, the monsoon season started again in I Corps. In our command center the main event was the completion of Operation Pipestone Canyon which started on 26 May 1969 with the objective to sweep the Dodge City-Go Noi island area. The operation lasted over five months and opened Route 4 to traffic from Hoi An to Dai Loc and further to Thuong Duc. In addition, the 1st Marine Division began augmentation of the Combined Action Program with rifle companies and Company M, 1st Marines sent squads into hamlets near Hill 55 to work with local Regional Forces and Popular Forces as the first one in the program. The Combined Action Program had grown during the year in our area to 1,710 Marines and 119 Navy corpsmen who made about 150,000 patrols, most of them at night, with the Vietnamese counterparts, resulting in 1,938 NVA KIA, 425 POW and 932 weapons captured. The year's goal of having 90 percent of the population secure in I Corps was reached in October and the percentage was increasing during the rest of the year. One spot report during my watch taught us that Combined Action Company Commanders should be very careful when scheduling troop inspections over the radio. A company commander was ambushed and killed on the way to an inspection which had been previously announced over the radio in the clear to everybody.

At the end of 1969, the operational tempo in our command center slowed down further. The third redeployment was scheduled to start in January and this time 12,900 Marines would be withdrawn from Vietnam. The 26th Marines would leave from west of Da Nang to go to Camp Pendleton for deactivation. The 1st Antitank Battalion would redeploy also since there were no NVA tank units facing us. The 1st Tank Battalion was scheduled to leave also minus one company of M-48 medium tanks who were deployed in the Da Nang rocket belt. The 1st Shore Party Battalion departed minus one company left to work on helicopter landing zones and the 3rd Amphibian Tractor Battalion minus six LVTH-6 tractors would also depart. Four tactical squadrons, three fixed wing and one helicopter, would go too as part of the third redeployment.

Before the redeployments, the III Marine Amphibious Force had included the 1st and 3rd Marine Division, the 26th and 27th Regimental Landing Team, a greatly enlarged Marine Aircraft Wing, the U.S. Army XXIV Corps Headquarters in Phu Bai, the 101st Airborne, 1st Cavalry and Americal Divisions, and the 1st Brigade, 5th Mechanized Division. After the 3rd Marine Division and its supporting units left, the Army had more troops in I Corps than the Marines. Therefore, on 9 March 1970, upon departure of Lieutenant General Nickerson as Commanding General of III MAF, the XXIV Corps became the senior command and moved to Da Nang. For operations, Marines had one division-wing team left with the 1st Marine Aircraft Wing assets coming increasingly under single management control of the 7th U.S. Air Force. The division-wing team was scheduled to be withdrawn to Camp Pendleton during the 4th and last redeployment in April-May 1970 clearing out all Fleet Marine Forces from Vietnam.

FAREWELL TO VIETNAM AND REDEPLOYMENT TO SUBIC BAY

In late November 1969, I carried out my orders and reported to the Subic Bay Naval Base in the Philippines, to become the I Marine Expeditionary Force and Fleet Marine Pacific Liaison Officer with the additional duty of Officer in Charge of the Special Landing Force Camp in Subic Bay. Since General Jones, Commanding General of I MEF, was my superior in the Personnel Department and awarded the Navy Commendation Medal with Combat "V" to me for my first tour of duty in Vietnam, it appeared likely that he had something to do with my assignment to the Philippines. His staff on Okinawa soon gave me a list of tasks that General Jones wanted done right away. First, the camp was to be refurbished for use by Marine battalions when not afloat off the coast of Vietnam. Second, training areas in Subic Bay were to be cleaned up and made ready for firing exercises. Third, beaches for amphibious landings were to be prepared. Fourth, hand-made cigars from Olongopo City were to be sent to General Lam in Vietnam with a band on each cigar saying "General Lam, CG I Corps". Lastly, a large Marine eagle, globe and anchor was to be made in Olongopo for the 3rd Marine Division Officers Club, paid for by club dues and delivered to Camp Courtney, Okinawa.

The Subic Bay Naval Base was commanded by Rear Admiral Lambert and consisted of a number of tenant commands. There was a large repair facility and a supply depot. The air station was commanded by Captain "Red" Meyers who was a World War II ace. The Marine Barracks was commanded by Colonel Edmondson. My office was near Admiral Lambert's command center and near the Philippine Constabulary Liaison Officer who worked on the ongoing Huk guerrilla problems which flared up sometimes. My staff consisted of three Marine sergeants and three pickup trucks were assigned to us. Somehow, everything that General Jones wanted was done with a lot of work and the help of the Navy. The camp was rebuilt with supplies sent from Vietnam by Admiral Elmo Zumwalt who was redeploying. When General Leonard Chapman, Commandant of the Marine Corps, came to inspect the camp in March 1970, he was pleased with the progress made. Brigadier General Barrow, Commander of Marine Bases on Okinawa, was also pleased when he visited the camp and training areas.

General L. Chapman, Commandant of the Marine Corps and
Rear Admiral C. Lambert, Subic Bay, March 1970.

On the less serious side, I also had some special projects to carry out. First, during the 7th Fleet Planning Conference, Rear Admiral Dipdal, Commander of Amphibious Forces Pacific, told me to check on the quality of food served aboard ship to Marines. The admiral had a brother who had been a Marine Private First Class during World War II and was demanding that the admiral provide good food to the Marines. Second, General Johnson came from Iwakuni and told me to report to him any Marine helicopter pilot who flew nurses or school teachers from Clark Air Force Base to Subic Bay for dates or parties. Lastly, when during dinner at the officers club several admirals and General Jones needed to talk business, I was asked by Admiral Rosenberg, Commander Submarines Pacific, to ask Mrs Rosenberg to dance. Apparently, Mrs Rosenberg had a way to taking over the conversation. In the end, when it came time for me to go home in April 1970, General Jones said that my sergeants and I had done well and he awarded the Navy Achievement Medal to me.

CHAPTER 7 –
THE COLD WAR IN EAST
GERMANY

HOW STALIN STARTED THE COLD WAR

According to the historian Jonathan Brent, Stalin felt that his grip on power was becoming less secure at the end of World War II and wanted an enemy threat to gain more absolute control. He laid the foundation for the Cold War by making America the number one enemy and by propagating a lawless system of conspiracy against his own government in which he assaulted all law. He conducted the anti-cosmopolitan campaign in 1948 and planned to deport Jews in the Soviet Union to Siberia. Stalin had Molotov's wife arrested and fabricated the Doctor's plot. He had the KGB and ten million informants working for him in the Soviet Union to keep control of the population. From 1918 until the death of Stalin in 1953, over 20 million people were sent to labor camps from which many never returned. From 1953 to 1987, about 15 million more people were sent to labor camps and many died.

In addition, about 30 million victims perished according to the "Black Book" (available at the Vilnius Museum of Genocide Victims) and the Greek Orthodox Church. The victims perished: (1) in the Civil War brought about by the Bolshevik Revolution, (2) the man-made famines for collectivization, (3) executions during repeated purges by Stalin, (4) genocide against certain nationalities which opposed communism, (5) ethnic cleansing for Russification of nationalities, (6) the war against Finland, and (7) the mass murder of Soviet soldiers, millions of prisoners and innocent civilians. Many records of atrocities have been destroyed and many archives are kept secret. Some journalists, like Gediminas J. Indreika in Chicago, have continued to do research about past events which are not always open to the public. For example, it is interesting to me that as Russia is exerting its influence on the Baltic states to control their oil and natural gas supplies, in Lithuania a leftist parliament passed a law prohibiting access to the Lithuanian branch of the Soviet KGB archives for seventy (70) years, to apparently protect members of parliament and others who may have skeletons in their closet.

Stalin believed that his best chance to be an absolute boss was in a nuclear crisis. He was always on guard and claimed that America was planning an internal blow against Russia with two nuclear bombs which would be fired from the US embassy in Moscow. He proclaimed that the US was going to attack him from the Sino-Soviet border and not from Germany. Stalin asserted that nuclear war was inevitable with America. After Stalin's death on 2 March 1953, Khrushchev, Beria and other successors continued the confrontations with America. Reportedly Brezhnev planned a first strike nuclear attack against America but was deterred by the US submarine retaliatory capability. The Soviets threatened us in Germany, Korea, Cuba, Vietnam and in other hot spots.

NAVAL REPRESENTATIVE, U.S. MILITARY LIASON MISSION TO THE GROUP OF SOVIET FORCES, EAST GERMANY

After Subic Bay, my next assignment was Assistant Operations Officer, Henderson Hall in Arlington, Virginia. My commanding officer was Colonel William Zaro with whom I served in the 1st Marine Division in Vietnam and the Operations Officer was Major Herbert Edson, the son of General Edson of "Edson's Raiders" fame of World War II. After only serving six months, I was asked if I would volunteer for a tour of duty in East Germany, where I was needed because of my language qualifications, as a replacement for an officer who had not been to Vietnam yet and had orders to go there. It did not seem right for me to question the orders and they arrived at the same time as the award of a second Navy Commendation Medal with Combat "V" for my second tour of duty in Vietnam. I was given a refresher course in Russian and some training at the Attache School which prepared me for service as a Naval Attache.

On 27 January 1971, I reported to the U.S. Military Liaison Mission to the Commander in Chief, Group of Soviet Forces, Germany and assumed the duties of Naval Representative. The main part of the Mission was in a large house in Potsdam where representational functions were performed while my quarters, administrative support and motor pool were in West Berlin. The Mission was commanded by Colonel Howard Richie, U.S. Army and Air Force Lieutenant Colonel David Colgan was the deputy commander.

My assignment as Naval Representative was guided by the Lieutenant General Huebner- Colonel General Malinin Agreement of 5 April 1947 which established Military Liaison Missions accredited to the Soviet and United States Commanders in Chief of the Zones of Occupation Germany. The provisions of Article 2 of the Agreement on Control Mechanism in Germany of 14 November 1944 provided the legal framework for the exchange of military missions accredited to their staffs in the zones and the following briefly summarized regulations: (1) The missions are military and not political missions. (2) They will be composed of air, navy and army representatives. (3) The missions will consist of fourteen officers and enlisted personnel. (4) The task of the missions will be to maintain liaison between both Commanders-in-Chief and their staffs. Last, (5) the missions will have the right to protect the interests of their nationals and make representations accordingly. British and French Military Liaison Missions were also established with the same rules.

As the Naval Representative, I was given one of fourteen Soviet identification cards issued to the Mission which allowed me to enter East Germany. I had freedom of movement as long as I followed the Soviet rules and restrictions set down for the Mission. Special license plates were issued by the Soviets for our cars and Colonel Richie gave some of the identification cards to our drivers. Sergeant Kelly was the first driver who worked with me and drove me to the Mission house in Potsdam from Berlin. He said that he drove Colonel Richie to several meetings with Colonel Grishishkin of the Soviet External Relations Branch in Potsdam and around the local Berlin area during which Colonel Richie constantly ate Tums antacid tablets to keep his nerves under control.

The problem was that the Soviets were all taught during the Cold War that the United States was their main enemy. The Commander in Chief of Soviet Forces in East Germany was General Ivanovskiy. The Chief of Staff was Lieutenant General Yakushin. During my tour of duty it appeared to me that the political officer was Major General Masherov and Major General Khodakovskiy was the Assistant Chief of Staff for Intelligence. The policy of General Ivanovskiy was to allow our Mission officers to travel in East Germany as long as we stayed away from all military activity and never came near his headquarters in Wunsdorf.

As the Naval Representative of the Mission of the main enemy to the Soviets, it soon became clear during my early trips with Sergeant Kelly why Colonel Richie needed Tums all the time. There were twenty-two Soviet divisions and six East German People's Army (Nationale Volksarmee or NVA) divisions in East Germany and any soldier who saw my car which had a small American flag on the license plate had to think if he should shoot, ram or try to detain me. At the same time, I had an incredible opportunity to see the enemy at the height of the Cold War first hand and close up.

During my 37 month tour in a hostile environment, I was able to observe communist forces, their equipment and tactics on a daily basis, becoming an expert on everything about them. I was able to conduct overt reconnaissance deep inside East Germany in spite of high-speed car chases, shootings and detentions. I had an intimate view of the Soviet lifestyle, their economic and political problems. Several times I also served as an interpreter and delegate in high-level meetings between commanders of the Soviet and American armies.

CONFRONTATION AND RAMMING BY SOVIET TROOPS

During early 1971, I was asked to visit the city of Wittenberg by my Mission staff since there were a lot of Soviet installations and vehicle parks there. As a newly assigned officer with a Soviet pass I needed to use my access to let them know what the Soviets were up to if possible. My first question was how do I find Wittenberg and since I had a camera body with several lenses if I should take a picture of the sights in the city. I was told to drive south on Route 2 and to use my camera discreetly bringing back any information I could without getting caught. If I got caught I was told that my Mission would claim that they did not know anything about it and the Soviets could terminate my accreditation.

My driver and I proceeded south from Potsdam on Route 2 thinking all would be well but we did not see about ten surveillance cars which were all around us. There were unmarked police and unmarked East German Army (NVA) cars along with regular People's Police (Volks Polizei - VOPO) cars following us all the time but being new I did not see any of them. As we approached Wittenberg, there were Soviet vehicle parks which could be seen partially from Route 2. I decided to turn left on a dirt road and to approach a vehicle park so that I could look at it better. My driver then told me that a Soviet UAZ-69 jeep was starting to follow us. We decided to get away from that vehicle when out of nowhere another UAZ-69 rammed the rear of our car causing considerable damage making it impossible to drive further.

Soviet soldiers armed with AK-47 assault rifles then surrounded us and an officer approached me and said that we were detained. He saw that I could not drive away without repairs and said that I would have to wait for further orders. He said that I was in a restricted military area behind a sign which said so and that charges would be prepared against me and the United States of America for a rude violation of the Huebner-Malinin Agreement and for spying against the people of the Soviet Union and East Germany. The officer said that he had to go back to his office but other officers would arrive soon.

The soldiers saw that my driver and I were unarmed and lowered their rifles after the officer left. My driver and I decided to offer them cigarettes and several cans of coca cola which they accepted and then I asked them to help repair the bumper and fender damage to my car so that I could move again. After looking around for any officers, with a heavy hammer from our trunk the soldiers banged the car back into shape and freed our rear wheels for movement. Soon a Soviet Colonel arrived and said that he was a legal officer with papers for me to sign in the Kommandatura (Provost Marshall's Office) in Wittenberg and a doctor would examine us for possible injuries. I said that I needed to go back to Potsdam for repairs and to see our own doctor for my driver and me for possible treatment. Further, I said that there was no injury to Soviet soldiers, no damage to the Soviet vehicles and my commander will sign the papers later. With the soldiers smiling I said to the Colonel that it was a pleasure to meet him but I need to go and since he hesitated to draw his revolver we backed up slowly towards Route 2. After a few seconds of moving the car without being shot at I told my driver to pick up speed. We raced back to Route 2 and drove at high speed away from the detention back to Potsdam.

PROVIDING EARLY WARNING FOR BERLIN AGAINST COMMUNIST TAKE OVER

After returning to our Mission house in Potsdam, we conducted more body work to the rear of the car and waited until dark before attempting to cross the Gross Gleinecke bridge Soviet check point to West Berlin. We did this to insure that the guards would let us back to West Berlin without questioning the damage to the rear of our vehicle which could be seen much better in the day time and could be cause to detain us for leaving a scene of an accident. Fortunately, the Soviets in Wittenberg did not put in a hold for us at the check point and the guards decided to let us go.

Upon return to our backup facility in West Berlin, I had to do a lot of paperwork which was sent up the chain of command. There were many lessons for me to learn from the experience but after having my back and shoulder checked, another driver and car were assigned to me and I was sent out into the Berlin local area for a two-day trip. My mission was to see what was going on in East Germany in the vicinity of West Berlin and to deliver the Stars and Stripes newspaper to the Soviet External Relations Branch in Potsdam if possible.

In essence, if the Soviets decided to seize West Berlin, they would have to move and position tank and motorized rifle units which I might observe during my trip. By reporting all Soviet activities that I observed to my Mission staff, I could provide early warning to West Berlin which would help the U.S. Army defend the city if need be. It became clear to me after driving near Krampnitz, Dallgow-Doebritz, Bernau and Juterbog, that the Soviets had seven divisions and the East Germans had one division garrisoned near West Berlin which could be deployed rapidly against the city. So much for the claim of American liberal reporters and politicians, that there was no Soviet threat.

The Huebner-Malinin agreement was signed when Soviet hostilities towards the Free World were not as overt and blatant as they became during the Cold War. While celebrating victory over Hitler and the Nazis the exchange of a 14-man team for liaison between Soviet and American zones of occupation was no problem. As the Cold War heated up, members of our Mission often felt the brunt of Soviet hostilities as they evolved. In America and the West, liberal professors, reporters and politicians preached support for Communist ideals and the Soviets. In Potsdam, our Mission experienced the real aggression and hostility of the Soviets towards Americans and the Free World.

West Berlin was an outpost of the Free World like South Korea and South Vietnam with constant Soviet threats and hostile acts directed towards it. Under the policies of containment and appeasement of the American liberal-left towards the Kremlin, the Soviets knew that their aggression and hostilities towards West Berlin and our Mission would not be challenged. The Kremlin was the center of a communist empire that spread class struggle and collectivism to West Berlin and all parts of the world. The countless victims of communism were largely ignored by the liberal news media, liberal left-wing politicians and social activists in America and the West. As the Naval Representative of the Mission, I witnessed the Soviet Empire at its height from behind the enemy lines with constant efforts to expand in Europe, Afghanistan and Vietnam.

LESSONS LEARNED AND BECOMING AN OUTSTANDING RECONNAISSANCE OFFICER

Soviet officer and East German Police at a detention site.

78

Detention and ramming of one of our reconnaissence vehicles,
East Germany, 1972.

According to my father, the establishment in 1917 by Vladimir Lenin and his Bolsheviks of a Marxist dictatorship in Russia was the main reason for unprecedented bloodshed and mass murders in almost every part of the world. From Europe to Asia, Africa and Latin America, hundreds of millions suffered the brutality of communist regimes. As a Naval Representative to General Ivanovskiy and his staff in Wunsdorf I kept in the back of my mind what my father said. After two tours of combat duty in Vietnam before my assignment, I seemed to have a different approach to the Soviets than some officers who attended American universities under the Foreign Area Studies Program. Professors at American universities with the exception of Richard Pipes, Lev Dobriansky and a few others taught communist propaganda according to the views of the Communist Party of the Soviet Union. Some officers who were assigned to our Mission came with views based on communist propaganda from such American universities.

DEPLOYMENT OF THE 10TH GUARDS TANK DIVISION TO THE LETZLINGER HEIDE

Had the Soviets and their Warsaw Pact allies decided to go to war during my tour with the Mission, I would have been one of the first people to have a hint of impending hostilities. One day I assumed duty to patrol in the Berlin local area just as a British team was leaving. The British officer pulled up to my car and said the gates to the Krampnitz installations had been opened and the Soviets were about to deploy. He added that it was up to me to determine where they were going and to follow them. I said I am on my way but was worried about how to follow a tank division since I had never done that before.

As my driver and I checked the roads, armed Soviet traffic regulators were posted at all intersections. Then BRDM (rkh) scout cars of the reconnaissance battalion excited an installation. As we drove north on a road from Neu Fahrland a serial of vehicles appeared behind us. Soon I knew that we would be detained if I did not find a place to hide. I decided that my best observation point would be near Wustermark along Route 5. Not finding a place of concealment we backed up our car into a large dung heap near a farm house about 500 meters from Route 5. Although the odor was unpleasant the cattle excrement on top of our car was excellent camouflage.

The vehicles behind us proceeded northwest on Route 5 and I was able to count and identify all twenty of them. Soon another serial of twenty vehicles appeared and more serials followed. At one point Soviet staff officers in three UAZ-69 jeeps used the dirt road of our farm to avoid the heavy traffic on Route 5 and came within fifty meters of our car. Fortunately, they only saw parts of our green painted Ford sedan under the cow excrement and did not believe that it could be an American reconnaissance vehicle. We held our breath but they never really looked into the dung heap and drove on. At the same time, serial after serial of vehicles passed in front of us. The troop movements continued all day and into the night. After dark we moved out of the dung heap to about 100 meters near Route 5 and continued to count and identify vehicles all night. Since I had to use my binoculars and could not write, I used a tape recorder into which I spoke as I observed. At about 0200 hours in the morning, the Free Rocket Over Ground (FROG) surface-to-surface missile battalion passed in front of us. At about 0500 hours, the movement of vehicles came to an end. All in all, after the tapes were debriefed I had observed 892 vehicles deploying from the Krampnitz area. I then checked some of the tactical routes and markers until it seemed to me that they had moved towards the large Letzlinger Heide exercise area and it appeared that there were no hostile intentions towards West Berlin or West Germany.

After observing the wheeled vehicles of the division, we checked all the railroad sidings near Krampnitz. All the sidings were full of military trains and strakes with flatbed railroad cars. The flatbed railroad cars were loaded with T-62 tanks and other tracked vehicles. From the side numbers on the turrets of the tanks, I was able to identify tanks of all three tank regiments being loaded out. The self-propelled artillery vehicles of the artillery regiment were also on strakes. The anti-aircraft regiment's self-propelled AA guns were loaded along with radar and support vehicles. My count in the sidings amounted to another 600 vehicles observed and I felt that I had enough information along with photography taken in daylight hours to go back to West Berlin and make a report. Lieutenant Colonel Colgan said to me when I returned that he could not believe that one could observe so many vehicles. In reply I said to him listen to my tapes and look at the photographs. The 10th Guards Tank Division had conducted an exercise deployment as part of their normal annual training cycle and I had never seen so many tanks and other military vehicles before at one time in my life.

NOT WELCOME IN DRESDEN AND ENTERING A MOTORCYCLE RACE

In early 1972, our staff wanted to know if the scheduled Soviet troop rotation was taking place in East Germany as announced in newspapers in Moscow. My driver and I were sent to Dresden in full uniform to stay in a hotel near the main railroad station to observe if new recruits with their hair cut short were arriving from Russia. We were always followed by police cars and unmarked surveillance cars in Dresden and it was impossible to get near the center of the city where my family, Eugenia and Erikas lived and survived the bombing on 13 February 1945. We tried to get into several hotels further from the center but were denied permission to stay by angry hotel managers.

After being turned away several times, we stopped in front of a hotel further away from the center of the city with several police cars with us. I walked into the lobby and said I wanted rooms for me and my driver if possible. The manager came and said he had vacancies but not for British and American military personnel because we destroyed the city in 1945. He added that since you killed thousands of innocent civilians in Dresden we cannot allow you to stay here and that is why no hotel will give you rooms. When I asked where Praeger street was he said there is no such street any more and the communists have rebuild the center giving new names to some streets and squares

We then found a hotel in the outskirts and drove around close to the center the next day until we saw new Soviet recruits in several places in

Dresden. As we left the city, police cars followed us onto the Autobahn and we decided to try to lose them by driving fast uphill. They were not able to keep up with our powerful Ford sedan driving their underpowered police cars. While we were out of their sight we pulled into a rest area hoping they would not see us when they came by. Several cars passed without seeing us but then they came back looking everywhere.

In order to avoid the police, I looked for a back road leading away from the rest area and saw a small trail leading down a slope. We decided to take the trail since it was the only way out and we had to move fast. We bounced down the trail slowly and felt relieved to be near the bottom of the slope where we turned right on a wide dirt road. Suddenly we saw motorcycles pass us on each side of the car and upon closer look the drivers all had large numbers attached to their clothes. We were relieved that they were not policemen and continued to drive on the road with them trying to figure out where we were. Soon we saw people on each side of the road cheering on the motorcycle drivers and we were being passed by more motorcycles when it dawned upon me that we were in the middle of a race.

We could not get off the road because there were ropes on each side to keep the spectators out of the way. Soon we saw more people in stands and judges in a booth with a large "finish" sign at the end of the race track. We picked up speed and drove through the finish line with the lead motorcycles. The spectators looked at us in amazement at first until some one yelled: "Look, look at the Americans!" Then they yelled: "Hurray for America" as we drove away from the race track and disappeared into a nearby village and there were no police cars behind us.

US VETERANS AND ESCORTING AMBASSADOR MYRON RUSH TO POTSDAM

During 1972, President Nixon and Secretary Kissinger were negotiating arms control agreements with the Soviets and tensions were reduced in Berlin. The US Ambassador to Germany Myron Rush came to Berlin from Bonn to meet with the Soviets in Potsdam. As the Naval Representative of our mission I was selected to escort the ambassador to Potsdam. Before driving to pick up the ambassador at the residence of the political advisor to Major General William Cobb, Commander of the U.S. Sector of Berlin, I had time in the morning and decided to have breakfast at the Harnack Officer's Club.

While at the club, I was joined by several U.S. Army World War II veterans from a tour group. They said that they had revisited old battlefields and units with which they served. They wanted me to hear their assessment although I said that I had only limited time. They said that the U.S. Army was so depleted by the budget cuts of the Democrat controlled U.S. Congress and the Vietnam war that if the Soviets attacked we could not get one squad of soldiers together to defend Europe. They said that readiness was at an all time low while the Soviets were advancing in the Cold War.

Secretary Kissinger said many years later, that after our withdrawal started in Vietnam, the U.S. Congress reduced economic and military assistance every year by 50 percent to Vietnam so that the Vietnam Air Force could not fly, the artillery had no ammunition and while the North Vietnamese communists sent 11 combat divisions south to attack Saigon, by congressional mandate U.S. aircraft carriers could not approach Vietnam to help. The Soviets were the winners in Vietnam as they took over Cam Rann Bay and gained a new sphere of influence.

After reporting to the house where Ambassador Rush was waiting, I was offered coffee and told that the ambassador would go alone with me to Potsdam where the Soviets were expecting us. Soon we were on the way and the ambassador asked me how things were going. I said that the Soviets had large modern forces in East Germany and their threat to the free world was real in my opinion. As we approached the Gross Gleinecke Bridge, I saw that all the gates were open. Soviet guards with rifles at present arms saluted our car and several limousines were waiting for the ambassador at the other end. The Soviets had many escort and East German police cars forming up into a line as the ambassador left my vehicle and got into a black limousine.

MOVEMENTS OF THE 4TH EAST GERMAN MOTORIZED RIFLE DIVISION NEAR ERFURT

During a three day reconnaissance of the southwest part of East Germany, the 4th East German Motorized Rifle Division (MRD) conducted exercises and many of its units left their installations. Columns of vehicles were on the Eisenach Autobahn and on nearby side roads. After observing the movements of units for several hours at different locations, my sense was that I needed to find an observation post away from the traffic and that I had been seen too much. A nearby hill with many pine trees on it seemed like an ideal location for an observation post.

We moved cross-country to the hill and backed our green painted Ford sedan into the trees at a point where we blended in with the terrain and had good concealment. We observed troop movements on several roads and the Autobahn for a number of hours from the observation post with no problem. Then I wondered how much longer I should stay since I had good photography, had identified and counted the units. Always looking in all directions and my rear, I felt protected by the pine trees which were planted in good German order a meter apart.

Thinking that no surveillance vehicles could harm me from the rear, I forgot that Soviet and East German reconnaissance battalions used motorcycle troops for advance and flank security. Seemingly out of nowhere, four East German soldiers with ES-250 motorcycles, with the engines turned off, were able to glide down hill between the trees behind me and before we could turn our engine on, surrounded us pointing their AK-47 Assault Rifles at us. Since I could not move, I decided to talk to them to diffuse the very tense situation to keep them from firing at us. I said good day in German and offered them some coffee saying that we were on a coffee break.

They hesitated for a moment but since my German was as good as theirs, they were surprised and lowered their weapons. They said that their commanders knew that we were monitoring their troop movements and sent them to confront us. They said the Soviets were coming to detain us soon but they would let us go if we moved before the Soviets arrived. After talking for a while with them, I thanked them and said it was a shame that an East German Borderguard Lieutenant was recently executed on the spot nearby for not killing three civilians who escaped to West Germany. Then I saw two Soviet GAZ-66 trucks loaded with armed troops heading our way across the fields. I wished the German soldiers the best and said that I better leave before the Soviets arrive. They smiled and we slowly pulled out of the tree line. I looked for a way to get to the Eisenach Autobahn and saw some dirt paths that looked tolerable. We picked up speed and the Soviets turned and tried to block us. After a short cross-country chase we left the two trucks in the fields and climbed on to the Autobahn from where we left the area at high speed.

CHECKING THE RAILROAD SIDING AT PRIORT

During early 1972, after some quiet tours of the Berlin local area where all units appeared to be in garrison conducting basic level training, my driver Sergeant Kelly and I continued to routinely check all railroad sidings. Although the Soviets had started their semi-annual training cycle at Krampnitz with new recruits who had arrived from the Soviet Union on Pendel troop trains and driver training was in progress, I knew that sometimes the Soviets conducted contingency war plan exercises at unexpected times. Since the Neu Fahrland siding was empty, I expected the Priort siding to be empty too but decided to check it anyway.

Sergeant Kelly and I hated to check the Priort siding since there was only one way in and out. To observe the siding one had to drive through the village, cross a bridge over a small stream and drive another 500 meters to get a good view. There were no traffic regulators and no troops in the village or near the bridge as we entered. I decided to proceed slowly for several hundred meters when we suddenly saw a Soviet tank regiment with 94 T-62 tanks and other vehicles loading out onto several military trains with flat cars.

As we observed the tanks, Sergeant Kelly told me to look in my rearview mirror which I adjusted and then saw Soviet soldiers forming into a road block in front of the bridge. The soldiers were pickets who had been lying along side of the road and we never saw them as we drove by. After we passed they got up, put their helmets on and formed up, with their AK-47s pointed at us, to block our escape. I photographed, counted and identified the tanks as Sergeant Kelly asked how to deal with the soldiers.

After some thought, I said let us approach them slowly and try to get back to the bridge. Our Ford sedan must have looked impressive to the soldiers with extra halogen lights, green paint over all chrome, tow hooks and a powerful V-8 engine because some in the center of the road started to make way as we approached. We smiled and I waived saying "comrade" as they ordered us to halt and pointed their weapons at us. I told Sergeant Kelly to point the car at the middle where they were giving way and said keep going slowly until they open up more. The game of chicken lasted a few seconds when one soldier in the center moved out of our way and I told Sergeant Kelly to pick up speed. I expected a burst of AK-47 fire as we broke through the line of soldiers but they did not fire and we were out of their range of fire instantly as we left them in a cloud of dust and gravel.

GETTING STUCK IN FRONT OF AN EAST GERMAN NAVY INSTALLATION

During June 1972, the weather was favorable for early morning photography and observation. In order to cover targets of naval interest, I had to go to the Baltic coast. The East German Navy had Soviet coastal defense missiles (Samlet) which could threaten NATO and U.S.ships in the Baltic Sea. It was my job to pinpoint the location of the missiles and find the installation where they were kept. After many previous trips to the area, I deduced that they were east of Rostock and I found the missile support facility where they were kept one early morning.

The facility was guarded and had elaborate security measures but my driver and I were able get close to it and to check it out. The best observation of Samlet missiles, associated transport vans and support vehicles was from the front of the main gate. Since it was very early, we were able to conduct our reconnaissance without alerting the armed sailors on guard duty until our Ford sedan got stuck in the sand. I did not realize how sandy the ground was near the coast and although we were only a few feet from the solid part of the dirt road our rear wheels were spinning in the sand without moving.

We had to use our winch from the trunk of the car. We tied a cable around an apparently strong tree and to the front of our vehicle. As we started to winch, we pulled the large tree out of its sandy foundation without moving the car. Next we used a large steel plate (called a "dead man") to provide support for the winch. We pounded six large metal stakes through the holes of the dead man into the dirt road in front of us. We hooked up the cable and the winch but the ground was too sandy there too and the dead man came out of the ground without movement of the car.

During a Reconnaissance Tour following tanks on a tactical route
during rainy weather, East Germany 1973.

By this time, the sailors on guard duty were fully alerted and one came over with his AK-47. I said good morning and when he saw the U.S. Marine

Corps globe and anchor on my cap his face turned white. He ran back to his post and sounded the alarm with a siren. At this point, we decided to use wooden boards (cheeta boards) under our rear tires. By digging under the tires we made enough room for the boards to provide traction. Although one board went flying into the air, the other board propelled the powerful Ford sedan back to solid ground and we were free to move.

Observing rail movements,
East Germany 1973

After we became mobile again, it was interesting to observe the commotion and turmoil on the missile base. Sailors without all their clothes on were running in all directions, some grabbing their weapons others opening vehicle sheds and starting vehicles to come out after us. My driver and I decided to calmly collect our dead man stakes, the dead man, winch, winch handle and large cable and to put it back neatly into our trunk. With one eye at the sailors, I then proceeded to cover our tracks with our entrenching tool and then we slowly drove away just as the sailors were about to come out after us. We accomplished our mission but unfortunately stirred up the installation in the process which I usually tried not to do.

BROKEN TIE ROD AND DETENTION AT DALLGOW-DOEBRITZ

After Colonel Frederick C. Turner replaced Colonel Howard Richie as Chief of Mission it seemed that the operational tempo improved. The frequency of my reconnaissance tours increased and I spent a lot of time in East Germany getting the information requested by the Mission staff. Along with more collection of information came more confrontations with the Soviets and East Germans. During early 1972, one tour in the local area was very productive but also frustrating. About twenty military trains passed one day through Wustermark with elements of the 1st and 8th East German Motorized Rifle Divisions on their way to the Letzlinger Heide training area. In order to photograph the trains, my driver and I had to go through several farms in order to reach overpasses and hills from which we could best see the movements. After many hours of observation, all the military trains had passed and we drove through a large field to leave the area.

As we reached the end of the field through which we were driving, we did not see a large rock covered by tall grass and we broke our right tie rod on it. We ignored the thump we heard and continued to drive successfully to the main highway. On the highway, we had difficulty controlling the Ford sedan and I told the driver to put both hands on the steering wheel thinking that it was his fault. Suddenly, the right front wheel collapsed and we skidded down a deep embankment on the right side of the highway. The car came to a halt about half-way down and was about to roll over when we climbed out through the driver's side door window to make it lighter and more steady. Farmers with two tractors were working nearby and I asked for help. A farmer with his tractor pulled our car back on the highway in return for American cigarettes and we pushed the car further along the highway.

We did not want the Soviets to know what had happened and cleaned up the embankment covering our tracks well. We called our Mission house for help and the duty sergeant drove with another car pulling a dolly to our aid. As we got our disabled vehicle on the dolly and were ready to leave, the Soviets arrived, blocked us in and detained us. The Soviet Officer in Charge and I argued for a while but in the end I had to accompany him to the Kommandatura at Dallgow-Doeberitz where he prepared papers with all kinds of charges. During the detention, we were offered coffee and accidentally I used the Lithuanian word "kava" in refusing the coffee. I was told that the correct Russian word was "coffee" and the word "kava" was only used in certain parts of the Soviet Union and by the way were did I learn the word "kava"? In reply, I did not want them to know that I was of Lithuanian origin and did some fast talking to change the subject. After several hours of discussion why I could not sign the papers I was allowed to go and return with our two vehicles to the Mission house in Potsdam.

SIGHTING OF SOVIET HELICOPTER REGIMENT
OVER PRITZWALK

During late 1972, on my way to Rostock, I decided with my driver to take a break and eat one of the sandwiches made by the East German staff at our Potsdam House for us. We were not far from Pritzwalk and while I observed the main highway, suddenly we heard helicopter engine noises. Usually we saw one or two helicopters, but this time there were many. I started to take photographs of medium HIP-C and large HOOK helicopters but ran out of film because apparently the whole regiment of over forty aircraft was flying south over my car.

The sighting of an entire regiment was of interest since we rarely saw large Soviet helicopter exercises in Germany. There were about ten HOOK and thirty HIP-C in the formation. They probably were returning to Altengrabow were their regiment was stationed. After I ran out of film in one camera, I used another camera with a smaller lens and was able to get panoramic photography of some of the formations at the end of the flight of helicopters. The pictures proved that the Soviet Tactical Air Army stationed in East Germany could conduct vertical envelopment operations similar to those of the U.S. Marine Corps and U.S. Army.

Upon returning to Berlin, I was happy to turn the pictures over to Major Lynn Hansen, Chief of the Air Team, in return for all the help given to me by the U.S. Air Force. Major Paul Nikulla, U.S. Air Force helped me to learn about the Soviets when I had first arrived and Staff Seargent, Nick Netter, U.S. Air Force was my driver sometimes. The sighting of the whole helicopter regiment in flight assisted them with their air order of battle assessments. Whenever possible I tried to get any information I could about the Soviet Tactical Air Army in East Germany to our Air Team. During my few conversations with Soviet officers, I was told that all information about the Soviet Air Force was secret and that in the Soviet Union even the snow was secret. At the end of the year, our Mission was awarded the Air Force Outstanding Unit ribbon and I was told that I was included in the award for my many reconnaissance tours in East Germany.

FLYING ALONG THE BERLIN WALL AS AN AIR OBSERVER

By my second year with the Mission, I had become an experienced reconnaissance officer knowing my way around East Germany without the use of maps. After nearly one hundred patrols through the same terrain, I concentrated on shortcuts and ways to do my work easier. By getting to know my Cold War enemies, I saved a lot of driving, confronting and grief. Having learned what tank and motorized rifle divisions do according to their annual training cycle, I often did not have to approach them and could tell from far away exactly what their readiness and activities were.

For example, once a year in April, almost all divisional anti-aircraft regiments fired their guns for qualification along the Baltic Coast. When I saw trains loaded with anti-aircraft guns, tracking radar and support equipment moving north, I did not follow them anymore. Instead, I drove north myself and waited at key railroad intersections, drinking coffee until I saw them again and checked them out. Then I left knowing that they were following their training schedules. I assumed also that the Soviets and East Germans would most likely not launch an attack through the Fulda Gap while all their anti-aircraft regiments were undergoing live fire training.

In the local Berlin area, I tried to find short cuts whenever possible when driving many miles day and night checking installations, railroad sidings, training areas and river crossing sites. Sometimes I missed some Soviet deployments and movements because I was at the wrong place. Once the 6th Guards Motorized Rifle Division moved out of Bernau while I was on the other side of Berlin and I missed their movement. One day Colonel Otto Chaney on our Mission staff suggested that I do what wealthy tourists do in Berlin and hire an aircraft for one hour to fly along the Berlin Wall. He suggested that I fly before my local trips to see what was going on. He was joking at first but after careful analysis of all the agreements, it appeared that I could save a lot of driving if I could fly as an Air Observer before my tours and if the U.S. Army would provide an aircraft.

Approval was gained from our Chief of Mission for an additional duty for me as a local air observer in the Berlin area. The U.S. Army agreed to provide an aircraft and I did not wear mission identification or travel in a readily identifiable Mission vehicle when proceeding to the aircraft in Berlin. Perhaps due at least partially to the subterfuge, the Soviets never raised any protest as I flew inside Berlin air space as an air observer before my ground reconnaissance tours identifying where military activity was and saving myself a lot of driving.

With the help of the U.S. Army pilots, I became very familiar with local conditions and garrisons in the immediate area surrounding Berlin. Sometimes, MiG aircraft challenged us and Soviet soldiers fired flare guns at us but we got the job done. My flights became routine and very helpful to my ground observations during reconnaissance missions. Since my flight log showed an accumulation of many hours as an air observer, I was proud of the air reconnaissance accomplishments and in my exuberance put in an informal request for Marine Corps air observer wings. However, my request was denied because I had not previously attended air observer school, was not on openly published flight orders and was not receiving flight pay.

MOVEMENTS BY THE EAST GERMAN 11TH MRD AND SCUD BRIGADE

During late 1972, after small unit training had been completed in many Soviet and East German divisions, large scale exercises were conducted. Although the East German 11th Motorized Rifle Division in Halle was not seen much by me before, on a day when I was checking the railroad siding at Schlettau there were flat cars with some of their vehicles and armed traffic regulators were posted everywhere. Before I could find a good observation post for the impending movements, the tank regiment deployed on a road in front of me and armed traffic regulators blocked and detained me in place.

My driver and I sat for eight hours in our car, as T-55 tanks, BTR-50s, ZSU-57-2s and many support vehicles passed in front of us. East German soldiers stood in front of our vehicle to block our view but I managed to get photography of the tanks anyway. When the movement ended a Soviet helicopter flew over our car but the Soviets did not come until a few hours later to present charges against me. I agreed to follow them to the Potsdam Kommandatura where a Soviet major read the charges. After I refused to sign the papers, I was released late at night in Potsdam.

A few days later, I returned to Halle and checked the dirt roads and training areas to assess the extent of the exercises. On the way to Schlettau, a Soviet lieutenant in a ZIL-131 workshop van decided to block my way and tried to detain me. My driver and I laughed to ourselves as we drove around the astonished lieutenant by going off the road and around his vehicle. Two Soviet soldiers pointed their AKMs at us but hesitated to fire for a moment and we were able to get out of their range with no problems.

During the remainder of 1972 and early 1973, I was able to conduct continuous reconnaissance tours without detentions until the East German Scud missile brigade move at Neubrandenburg. Our Mission received a tip that the Scud brigade would be in Neubrandenburg at a certain time and I was selected to observe what was going on there. With Sergeant Charles Krutz as the driver, we proceeded to Rostock first and as if by coincidence approached our target area when we encountered two Peoples Police motorcyclists who apparently were waiting for us and immediately began pursuit.

As we entered Neubrandenburg on a two-lane road, we passed through two traffic control posts and picked up in succession another police motorcyclist, three Peoples Police sedans and two State Security (MfS) sedans. The sedans and motorcyclists attempted to box us in and block our way. As we entered the ring road of the city, we had wanted to go left (north) as the Scud missiles were only about 100 meters away but a motorcyclist moved up to the left front wheel and prevented us from turning left. We then continued straight through traffic toward a park with a large fountain hoping the motorcyclist would drop off. At the last moment we had to make a right turn but the motorcyclist kept going straight, hit the fountain wall and flipped into the fountain. The remaining security vehicles then became extremely reckless in their pursuit and tried to ram us. In order to prevent injury to civilians walking in the streets and possible loss of life, I decided to slow down and face the detention. At the same time, a W50L militia truck came at us head on and in seconds the other vehicles boxed us in. Then policemen with guns drawn surrounded us. The next few minutes were tense as the policemen were young, agitated and not sure of their orders, until state security officers regained control over the situation and began managing the detention. After three hours, a Soviet officer arrived and demanded that we accompany him to the Soviet headquarters at Neustrelitz. While at Neustrelitz, we were subjected to a lengthy interrogation, an accusation of spying and demand to sign a written confession. After continued refusal to sign the confession we were released to return to Berlin.

LEANING FORWARD DURING LARGE SCALE MOVEMENTS

Training cycles for most Soviet units ended with large-scale exercises after which many soldiers were rotated home to be discharged into the reserves. During the exercises, units usually moved on several axis on many tactical routes using pontoon bridges hastily constructed over rivers. When bridges could not be constructed in time, Soviet tanks were equipped with snorkels and drove under water through river bottoms some-times. In order to determine the nature of the exercises, we had to get close enough to see what was going on. Sometimes, not knowing the extent of the movements, my drivers and I leaned forward and charged through the exercise areas until we found observation posts or a temporary place to hide if we were being pursued.

Leaning forward during troop movements,
East Germany, 1973.

On four trips with Sergeant Charles Krutz, we surveilled 667, 862, 198 and 75 Soviet vehicles respectively. At other times with Sergeant William Lear and other drivers we made similar observations. The Soviets took aggressive counter-measures to capture or ram us but we avoided detentions by knowing the terrain and using the speed of our powerful Ford vehicle to get away. On one occasion, we pulled off a highway onto a small dirt road to hide for a few minutes, when several Soviet reconnaissance vehicles came down the road behind us. They surrounded us and an officer said that we were on a tactical route on which many vehicles would come and he had to detain us. I said that I did not know that, after approaching his scout car. While I kept him talking, we were then able to get away through an opening between two BTR-60P armored personnel carriers.

During late 1972, while covering movements from Route 5, our vehicle was side-swiped by West German students who fell asleep and lost control of their car. I saw their car coming at us while out of control and we came to a complete halt on the right side of the road. We waited until the car sideswiped us and bounced into a ditch behind us. Soon the Soviets arrived and immediately charged me with causing an accident while spying on Soviet military movements. I said I was hit while halted and while talking to them decided to suddenly leave before they could box me in with more vehicles, which were arriving. In mid-1973, in the same area while observing Soviet columns, a Soviet MMZ-555 trash truck came at us at high speed from our rear with the intent of ramming our vehicle. We pulled away from the truck just in time and after catching our breath found a better observation post.

Many years later, after the Berlin Wall came down and Germany was reunited, the German government released the personnel file that the communist Ministry for Security (MfS) kept on me. The communists said in the file, that during 1971-1974, I was an official member of a military USA secret service, a member of the reconnaissance department of the U.S. 7th Army and chief of the Navy section of our Mission. The communists said in the file they kept on me that the main points of my reconnaissance activity were: railroad sidings, Soviet Army and East German Army columns, rockets and communications objects, airfields and training areas of the USSR and NVA. The communists added in the file that I demonstrated high risk-taking readiness as well as extremely provocative vehicle operation.

PROVING THE PRESENCE OF SOVIET NUCLEAR WEAPONS

In mid-1973, I led a three man operation into Wittenberg, with Sergeant Peter Samuelvich as the driver and Major Thomas Spencer as the operator of special equipment in the back seat which could detect the presence of nuclear weapons. Our mission was to verify the presence of tactical nuclear weapons with Soviet forces in the forward area since some members of Congress and news media claimed that the Kremlin was peace loving and not a threat to Europe. Left-wing Democrats demanded proof as to why money should be spent on defense when the Soviets and their communist allies announced their peaceful intentions to the world.

Our objective was to get the radiation detection equipment next to Soviet weapons or installations to get a reading of what was really there. The detection equipment was taken by Army and Air Force officers of our Mission on operational tours with marginal readings in most cases or negative results. The problem was that Soviet forces kept nuclear weapons under tight security. Soviet FROG-7 and SCUD missiles were rarely seen and kept hidden from NATO and western observers. The communists played the American news media and the Democratic Party like a violin demanding that we withdraw from Berlin and Europe. American liberals, socialists and communists echoed the Kremlin's party line claiming that there was no Soviet nuclear threat to Berlin or Europe.

In the early evening, we drove into Wittenberg with the intent of checking on the 6th Guards Tank Division that was due to return from large-scale exercises. Driving south on Route 2, we first saw civilian vehicles backed up and then halted on the highway. I gave the order to pass the halted vehicles and Major Spencer turned on the detection equipment just in case it was needed. As we proceeded, we saw armed Soviet traffic regulators and UAZ-469 jeeps with flashing blue lights. Then we saw a GAZ-66 truck with armed troops and two MAZ-537 low-bed trucks, each with a tarped SCUD-A missile launcher vehicle on its low-bed. Several command and security vehicles were in the front of the column.

Major Spencer said the equipment in the back seat was working. I told Sergeant Samuelvich that we would pass the whole column and that we wanted to get our equipment (now in the right rear seat) as closely to the tarped vehicles as possible. I added that I would conduct night photography with our lights, our high-beam lights and two special halizone lights in the front of our vehicle all turned on at the same time. I said this because through my binoculars, I saw two oxygen bottles protruding from under the tarping and knew from many hours of studying ID photographs that the oxygen bottles were a signature for the SCUD-A.

We ran the whole column, were able to get our equipment within several feet of the SCUD-A and I was able to photograph the missile launchers. After about 800 meters, we turned right into a dark street at a point where streetlights were illuminating Route 2. With the help of the streetlights, we photographed the column again and turned our detection equipment on again as the column passed in front of us. Then we broke our position in the dark and passed the column again to make sure we had accurate readings and good photography.

My plan was to drive south on Route 2 at high speed and out of the city. We needed to cross a double rail line to get away but the cantilever gate at the rail line had been lowered to block our escape and we were surrounded by Soviet troops with four vehicles. The troops pointed their AKM assault rifles at us until we turned off our engine. We were detained all night but I insisted that only I would leave the car at the Kommandatura to hear the charges and accusations. The chief of staff of the 6th Guards Tank Division said to me that I had endangered the lives of civilians and I should confess that I was nothing but a common spy (nastayashchii shpion). In reply I said that I was no spy because I wore my uniform and my car had the American flag on its license plates. I also said, that whatever they think I did to their military column is nothing compared to what the KGB and GRU do in Berlin and Europe. After all the charges were read to me the Soviets added a compliment saying that my conduct during the detention had been tactful. After sitting all night in a chair in their conference room at about 7:30 AM they received a phone call from Wunsdorf and told me that I was free to leave.

We returned to Berlin where the developed film showed indeed SCUD-A launchers and the readings from our detection equipment were sent to Washington. Many years later, on 6 January 1997, our Chief of Mission wrote in an award recommendation to the U.S. Army in accordance with a new law giving him permission to do so, that the debriefed readings of our detection equipment confirmed the presence of Soviet nuclear weapons in the forward area from residual radiation found on the SCUD-A. Our Chief of Mission added that he was personally thanked by high-ranking officials in Washington for the results of this and other missions conducted by me.

VISITING CINCUSNAVEUR IN LONDON AND THE BRITISH ARMY OF THE RHINE

Before assuming my assignment in Berlin, I was told that I should pay a call on Admiral Bringle, Commander in Chief, U.S. Navy Europe (CINCUSNAVEUR) during the middle of my tour to let him know how I was doing. Our Mission gave me one day to visit London after I got on the admiral's schedule to give a short slide briefing to the admiral and his staff. The slides were made from photographs which I took in East Germany of Soviet and East German military equipment, training areas, railroad sidings and installations. When I was all set up to brief in the conference room, the admiral came in along with members of his staff and said that he did not know that we had a Marine in Berlin and told me to proceed with the slides. After the briefing Admiral Bringle said that he had two visitors calling on him that day. One visitor was General Goodpaster and the other was I, the Naval Representative from Berlin. The admiral then complimented me on the briefing and work I was doing, adding that what I had to say was the most interesting thing he heard all day and my visit was by far more interesting than that of General Goodpaster, the Supreme Allied Commander of Europe (SACEUR). A few months later, I was asked to come back to brief Admiral Bagley, who was Admiral Bringle's replacement, which I did.

On 7 October 1973, I was selected by our Mission staff to fly from Berlin to Rhein-Dalen for one day upon the invitation of the Commander, British Army of the Rhine, to give my slide briefing there. The staff in Rhein-Dalen let me set up my slides for the briefing in one of their conference rooms but no projectionist was at first available and then the corporal who showed up decided with British humor to turn some of my slides in the tray upside down for fun. My briefing was well received although I had to stop several times to ask that the slides be corrected. After the briefing a Brigadier General thanked me and said that he was the G-2 Intelligence Staff Officer of the British Army of the Rhine but he could not recognize any of the Soviet equipment in my photographs. He added that he just arrived from Singapore where he had commanded the ANZEC Brigade (Australian-New Zealand-English Combined Brigade) and he could not tell one piece of Soviet equipment from another. I said that for the first months in Berlin I had the same problem.

After the briefing, I was invited to the officers club for some drinks when my name was called over the intercom at the bar. I asked if they maybe had a Major Nargele in the British Army when my name was called again and several officers said no. They laughed and said that I was being paged and that NATO forces had just gone to a DEFCON 3 readiness condition which meant that everyone at the bar was getting their helmets and rifles. As I walked to the entrance, a British Army woman corporal saluted me and said that she was ordered to drive me to the airport immediately to catch a flight back to Berlin. She gave me five minutes to get my gear and then drove me at high speed through red traffic lights and angry Germans to an airliner which took me back to Berlin.

OBSERVING THE POLISH BORDER DURING THE OCTOBER 1973 MIDDLE EAST WAR

Upon returning to Berlin from Rhein-Dalen, I was met by an officer from our Mission at the airport. He said that we were at the DEFCON 3 readiness condition because the October 1973 Middle East War had started when Syria and Egypt launched a surprise attack against Israel on 7 October with many new weapons provided by the Soviet Union. The Kremlin had sent the Soviet Black Sea Naval Infantry Brigade to Syria along with several warships and Soviet Airborne Divisions were moving towards the Middle East.

The officer from our Mission said that I had been ordered to proceed to the Polish border to observe if Soviet forces were moving into East Germany from Poland. A car and driver were waiting for me with my field jacket and equipment, extra rations and water ready to go. The officer added that the situation was very tense and that I should be careful not to get detained. Within one hour, my driver and I were crossing the Gross Gleinicke Bridge into East Germany and we saw signs everywhere of preparations for possible war.

My driver and I talked about what back roads we might use until nighttime. We drove through hamlets and small villages on farm roads and forest trails until we were forced onto Route 9 by the terrain. There was still plenty of daylight as I looked ahead on the two-lane hard-surface road with my binoculars and saw an entire Soviet artillery regiment coming our way from Cottbus. They had just left their barracks on a crash basis because many soldiers were still adjusting their gear, helmets and uniforms while moving to their pre-designated alert positions. My driver and I smiled and waved as we passed the entire regiment going the other way. While smiling we were able to take photographs of ZIL-131 trucks towing D-30 122mm howitzers and other vehicles. The officers were in too much of a hurry to detain us and let us get by.

After the sun went down, it was easier to escape and evade our way to our objective area at the Polish border. We got there at night and observed a major rail line along with two highways between Poland and East Germany for three days. We used a camouflage net which we brought with us, a lot of branches and foliage and somehow managed to remain undetected. On the third day, I had been told to report back and we returned to Berlin after having seen no Soviet troop movements. I was complemented by our staff for having observed the border and having confirmed that the Soviets were not preparing to attack in Europe. That information was needed by the Pentagon and the White House, I was told later, to allow the U.S. forces to stand down in Europe.

Many years later, it was explained to me that my observations about Soviet movements, new equipment, installations and training were of critically high value to US national security both in the ultimate US/NATO winning of the Cold War and to actual war fighting with the Soviet bloc had that been necessary. My reports sometimes were sent straight to the White House where they were marked as most reliable because I backed up my observations with photography and was a commissioned officer of the United States Marine Corps on the scene of the events. Many other reports to the Pentagon and the White House were unreliable because they came from double agents, the diplomatic cocktail circuit or other dubious sources. When I reported that no Soviet second echelon forces were moving to East Germany from Poland on one of the most important rail lines and two important highways during the October 1973 Middle East War it was of great value to policy makers I was told. The weather in October blocked out satellite coverage of the area and the most reliable information came from me because I drove to the area, personally observed the border and took photographs as proof.

From personal experience, other officers who served in Potsdam attested years later, to the high risk of bodily injury taken by me in collecting intelligence information in the hostile environment of the Soviet occupied territory of East Germany. Agents of the Soviet KGB, the East German Ministry for State Security (MfS), VOPOS or Volkspolizei (People's Police) and Soviet/ East German armed security guards were constantly taking aggressive hostile action to prevent members of our Mission from collecting information on their forces. The success in intelligence collection achieved by me was attributed by senior officers afterwards directly to my skill, daring, personal valor, courage, devotion to duty, professional knowledge and disregard for my own safety. At the time, it was very gratifying to me that my accomplishments provided nearly one third of the justification for the award of the Army Meritorious Unit Commendation to our Mission. In retrospect, we were not really much of a liaison mission but instead we were a reinforced reconnaissance platoon always out front covering East Germany for the US Army in Europe and serving behind the front lines of the Cold War.

GOING INTO GUARDED INSTALLATIONS AND TRAINING AREAS

In order to observe the readiness and any upgraded capabilities of Soviet forces, as requested by our policy makers in Washington, it was sometimes necessary to enter training areas and even installations at the risk of being shot or rammed. The difficult and often impossible assignments given to us sometimes required the taking of calculated risks after a lot of advance research and planning. We used to say that we could do the difficult requirements right away and the impossible ones would take a little longer.

Some training areas were not well marked and it was possible to enter them and then drive around without knowing how close one was to a sensitive location. In early 1973, with Sergeant Krutz as the driver, we attempted to surveil an installation near Ludwigslust, where a Soviet independent tank regiment was stationed which tested new tanks and other vehicles on a nearby driving range. Some T-64 tanks had been first tested there before they arrived in larger quantities to the forward area. The installation was not well marked and was near the same spot where 12 years later US Army Major Arthur Nicholson, a member of our Mission, was shot and killed by Soviet sentries.

As we slowly proceeded in our vehicle along a forest trail to get a look at the back of the driving range, a Soviet soldier appeared in front of us. When we began backing away, soldiers appeared behind us. The soldiers tried to block our way until the arrival of Soviet vehicles. It dawned on me that we had entered a much more sensitive part of the test area than I thought. By slowly pushing one soldier away we were just able to escape as two BTR-60P armored personnel carriers were approaching.

In late 1973, Colonel Otto Chaney, US Army, our operations officer at the time, issued a warning order to me, to plan for and be ready to conduct, a vehicular photo-reconnaissance operation against an alternate Soviet army command post installation. I was told that a requirement had existed for months to conduct such an operation but none of our officers were able to do it during their trips to the area because of the security measures there and armed guards.

The alternate command post consisted of about fifty bunkers, forty communication junction boxes, a communication center and some administrative buildings. The installation was enclosed by a double chain-link fence with three strands of barbed wire on top. A guard shack was at the main entrance which was manned by armed guards and the guards patrolled the area.

The requirement issued to us by an intelligence agency in Washington, asked that we enter the installation if possible, photograph the inside of the communication center and junction boxes, get pictures of all equipment and call signs along with pictures of all the bunkers. Colonel Chaney told me that he thought that I was the best and most experienced reconnaissance officer and selected me to lead a three-man team into the installation to photograph what was required and hopefully get out without being seen by the guards.

As I began planning the operation, Colonel Chaney specified that the best chance of success was on New Year's Eve when Soviet soldiers were known to drink vodka to break up the boredom and keep warm in the cold weather. After I prepared and submitted the plan for approval, I was surprised by the leadership of Colonel Chaney and his policy of going along on tough missions himself. He said the team would consist of Sergeant Peter Samuelvich as the vehicle operator/reconnaissance driver, Colonel Chaney in the back seat with the job of photographing everything I photographed a second time and me as the commander of the team and the operation because of my three years of experience as a reconnaissance officer and my familiarity of the area which I surveiled several times before.

To reinforce the importance of the intelligence requirement and the operation, Colonel Chaney asked me to come to the office of the Chief of Mission, Colonel Frederick C. Turner, US Army. We briefed Colonel Turner about the plan and after some apparent soul searching he told us to go ahead. In addition, it was decided after the completion of the operation to attempt to satisfy an additional tasking, to locate elements of an East German Scud Brigade, reported to be training in large training area north of Dresden.

The operation order included a cover and deception plan. Colonel Chaney and I had to appear in dress uniform for dinner at the US Army Harnack House officers club where waiters and Soviet spies most likely reported our presence. After a while during dinner, we suddenly departed through a back door and returned to our office, where we changed into utility uniforms. Sergeant Samuelvich was waiting with our vehicle and equipment ready to go. We left West Berlin and crossed the Gross Gleinecke bridge checkpoint at about 11:00 PM.

In East Germany, we avoided the normal check-in at our official residence house in Potsdam. We drove at high speed for about two hours on the autobahn and arrived safely without surveillance at our first stand-off observation post (OP) which was about 30 kilometers from our objective. There Sergeant Samuelvich and Colonel Chaney slept for about two hours while I stood watch. I was too anxious to sleep myself and stayed awake on guard for any possible surprises. After all was quiet, at about 4:00AM, we displaced to our second stand-off OP which was about 5 kilometers from our objective. After waiting for about an hour, my light meter readings off the hood of our car began to justify moving to our last stand-off OP. I gave the order to displace to a tree-covered hill overlooking the target, which was our last stand-off OP.

As soon as we had a minimum of daylight for low-light photography, I commenced the operation. We broke our tree cover and drove cross-country over frozen fields. The ground was solid like the autobahn because of the very cold weather. There was only one two-lane, hard-surface road between us and the front gate of the target. As I was watching the front gate through my binoculars for any sign of sentries, a Volga staff car appeared on the road in front of us. The car was full of East German army officers who were drinking wine from bottles they had in their hands and as they passed from right to left in front of us they saw us.

Colonel Chaney said not to cancel the operation because he thought the officers would not report us and our vehicle. I told Colonel Chaney, that as long as I was in charge and based on my three years of experience, we had at the most ten minutes to get in, photograph the installation and get out.

We slowly approached the front gate. The sentries were all in the guard house which was about 100 meters from the front gate. Lights were visible through the windows and smoke came out of the chimney of the guard-house. I got out of the car and quietly opened the front gate. Sergeant Samuelvich drove the car into the installation and turned it around to facilitate escape. I ran to each bunker, the communications center and each junction box, photographed the inside, with Colonel Chaney with me at all times, photographing everything a second time, before I closed each of the doors and each of the boxes. My hands were shaking so badly when I had to change film that I had to stop myself from shaking and had to calm myself down in order to be able to do it. I watched the door of the guard-house with one eye as I photographed everything. The car doors were open, our car engine ran quietly, and we were prepared to dive into the car at any moment if the sentries came out.

Miraculously the sentries remained in the guard-house, perhaps because of the cold weather or due to vodka drinking. After closing the last box, we photographed the lanes leading to the bunkers and rest of the installation. I asked Colonel Chaney to get into the car and with pine branches covered all our tracks with snow. I walked behind the car, as Sergeant Samuelvich drove it slowly out the gate. I closed the gate and then saw vehicle headlights in the distance moving toward us.

I jumped in our vehicle and directed Sergeant Samuelvich to follow the main dirt road leading away from the front gate towards the autobahn. Soon we could see a Soviet four-vehicle column coming toward us and the front gate. Our vehicle was painted dark green with no chrome showing. We were partially concealed by the fog which had developed and we kept our headlights off. The dirt road improved into a two lane road and was our best chance for escape. We picked up speed as I could see two UAZ-469 jeeps and two GAZ-66 trucks loaded with troops and driving fast in the right lane. I told Sergeant Samuelvich to floor it, as the column passed us, and the last vehicle came to a screeching halt. Our car began to reach high speed as we escaped to the autobahn. We drove at great speed for about four hours to the large training area north of Dresden and searched it for the elements of a Scud brigade with negative results. We made it back in the evening to West Berlin.

COMMENDATIONS, HOSPITAL VISIT AND ADMIRAL RIVERO VISITED BERLIN

Upon return to West Berlin, Sergeant Samuelvich and I were commended according to Colonel Chaney in evaluations of the information we collected. Colonel Chaney told me not to talk about our operations for a decade or so afterwards since no one needed to know about them. Colonel Chaney added that if we tried to tell others about some of our operations they would not believe what we accomplished anyway and would say that such operations were not unusual, done by others better or just as well in other places and at other times. The Soviets disagreed, however, in their protests to our Chief of Mission and our State Department. The Soviets knew that we had collected well against them only they did not know how well. My name was mentioned in long dispatches with considerable anger and threats of action against me for confrontations, escapes from detention and brushes with Soviet troops. Colonel Turner asked Colonel Niunin of the Soviet External Relations Branch about me before writing my final fitness report and said that the KGB Colonel became so angry that they had to change the topic of conversation.

The direct confrontational events during operations took their toll on my physical and mental health. During my third year, I had shingles, bruises, internal bleeding and it seemed that the adrenalin stopped coming out of my eyes before roadblocks and guns pointed at me. When I made a visit to the US Army Berlin hospital they conducted various tests and declared me 4F which meant I was unfit for active duty. Not knowing what to do, I called the Marine Barracks in London. After discussion with Marine administrators, I decided that I had to last in my job until my tour of duty was over and I was relieved by Lieutenant Colonel John Guenther. I therefore bought a case of Scotch which helped to reduce the pain of the shingles and conveniently lost the medical records which had declared me unfit for duty. When I was asked to extend by Colonel Turner, I extended for only thirty days due to my poor health.

At the same time, I was invited for dinner to the residence of Major General William Cobb, Commander of the US Sector of Berlin, because Admiral Horatio Rivero who came to Berlin wanted the senior naval officers present. Admiral Rivero was the Commander in Chief, NATO Forces South, with his headquarters in Naples and wanted to see what we were up against in Berlin. Commander John Gallagher and I were the only naval officers in Berlin at the time and we were invited. During the evening, I decided to mention the Cuban Missile Crisis to the Admiral and how I had served under his command but I did not mention that I failed to fly the absentee penant when he came to the USS York County to pick up our captain.

On several occasions the Soviets conducted social functions in Potsdam to which we were invited along with the French and British military mission members. During one such function Lieutenant General Yakushin asked my Chief of Mission after looking at my Marine Corps dress blue uniform if I belonged to the US or the British Mission. When he was told that I belonged to the US Mission, Lieutenant General Yakushin said he liked the Marine Corps uniform and told me that he knew where I was from. He said that I was from the 7th Fleet to which I replied that he was right, of course.

During one function hosted by us for the Soviets at our Potsdam house, I had to translate for Major General Hughes, the US Army Surgeon General in Europe who came from Heidelberg to Potsdam with several other flag officers. We were seated next to Major General Khodakovskiy who gave Major General Hughes a hard time over male nurses in the US Army. The Soviet general said that his soldiers when wounded like to be cared for by women nurses and do not want to be touched by male nurses who are in the US Army a reflection of perversion, drugs and a permissive capitalist society.

The Soviet general then told us two stories and one revealed that he was probably the Assistant Chief of Staff for Intelligence in Wunsdorf. He said that during World War II he conducted intelligence collection and reconnaissance and had to make a report to a commander who was an alcoholic. After traveling on a lot of dusty roads, Khodakovskiy asked his commander for a drink of water from a pitcher on a table in a tent before making his report. The pitcher looked crystal clear and appeared to be filled with water. The commander said go ahead enjoy it. Khodakovskiy filled a big glass and drank the whole content in one gulp only to start choking badly because the pitcher was filled with vodka and not with water. The other story was that Khodakovskiy was invited to a US buffet dinner once and saw near the center of the buffet table a bowl with silver foil wrapped objects. Thinking that the silver foil wrapped objects were a special American delicacy he took one but was disappointed because it was a baked potato.

During 1973, the Soviets gave a reception in Potsdam to honor the October 1917 Revolution which I had to attend. A Soviet Colonel who recognized my Marine Corps evening dress uniform greeted me and said that he worked in Wunsdorf and knew that there was a Marine division in North Carolina. He said that the Soviets were not afraid of the Marine division since they had many tank, motorized rifle and airborne divisions in the Soviet Army but they were very much afraid of the Marine Corps Radio Battalion which had a company stationed at Bremerhaven and monitored all Soviet military transmissions.

AUFWIEDERSEHEN, FAREWELL AND DO SVIDANIYA

In early 1974, as I was waiting for my orders home after only extending for 30 days to 1 March because of my poor health, the US Air Force Team of our Mission presented me with a beautiful parchment signed by the team's officers and NCOs. The parchment contained pictures of the New Gate and Sans Souci castle in Potsdam along with the Berlin Airlift monument at Templehof and our Potsdam mission patch. It meant a lot to me to have the signatures of the following on the parchment: W. Waltman, Bill Burhans, Lynn Hansen, Larry Patterson, T. Galbreath, Bob Ash, Gerald R. Rickey, Loren Allen, Gregory B. Cook, J.O. Donnell, Nichelaus G. Netter, Charlis Stitens, J. Lousipiart, Paul Hendricks and Eunnis Stubene. It made me sad that my friend Major David Hall, US Air Force, who had been caught outside his car by a Soviet airfield security platoon and had been beaten up by them was not with the Mission anymore.

Then Brigadier General Robert D. Stenins, USA, Commander Berlin Brigade, presented me with a picture map of divided Berlin showing the wall, the major buildings and the barbed wire fences around the free part of the city. The inscription on the map stated that having lived in Berlin and having guarded the freedom of the city I was awarded the map of the divided city as a symbol of my dedicated support for the cause of freedom.

Mrs. White was the Head of the Marine Corps Awards and Decorations Branch in Washington at the time and she sent me the Navy Occupation Medal for my service in Berlin which was still an occupied city in which we were performing occupation duties in addition to everything else. She told me that I had been awarded the Meritorious Service Medal and General Cushman, Commandant of the Marine Corps, wrote a special cover letter of endorsement for the citation. The citation stated that I had been awarded the medal for meritorious service in the performance of extremely difficult and often hazardous duties. Through the entire period, from 27 January 1971 to 1 March 1974, it was written that I had demonstrated outstanding courage, perseverance, sound judgment and great determination. It was stated that my distinguished performance of duty contributed substantially to the accomplishment of the unit mission and my achievements reflected great credit upon myself and the United States Marine Corps. The award was signed by General Michael S. Davison, Commander in Chief, United States Army Europe and Howard H. Calloway, Secretary of the Army.

After my service in Berlin, I was sent to Quantico, Virginia. From there I was ordered to the 3rd Marine Division in Japan and Korea. Then I served in the Pentagon and my last tour of duty before retirement was in the Dominican Republic. Since I knew that others were continuing to serve with our Mission in Berlin, I was worried for their safety knowing that I was lucky while in harm's way and others might not be so lucky. In 1984, I flew from Santo Domingo with a sense of foreboding to Berlin. I paid a call on Colonel Roland Lejoie, USA, the Chief of Mission, and talked to the reconnaissance tour officers. They wanted to hear about my experiences and after giving them some tips, I urged them to be careful when leaning forward. I had a very pleasant conversation and talked at length with Major Arthur D. Nicholson, Jr. before I left Berlin.

On Sunday, 24 March 1985, Major Nicholson left our Mission house with his driver, Sergeant Jessie Schatz, on a routine reconnaissance tour of the Ludwiglust area, the location of an independent Soviet tank regiment. At about 4:00PM, Major Nicholson left his car to walk to a tank shed to take pictures through a window. A Soviet soldier appeared and fired three rounds from his AK-47 rifle. One round hit Major Nicholson. When Sergeant Schatz tried to help Major Nicholson, Soviet soldiers stopped him. Major Nicholson then slowly died during the next hour before a Soviet medical orderly arrived. The next day, an ambulance was used to deliver Major Nicholson's body to a US Army honor guard at the Gross Gleinecke bridge check point. After several weeks, the Soviets finally apologized for the shooting but of course denied any responsibility.

A handwritten memorandum of 26 March 1985 by Comrade Lieutenant General Neiber, Division Chief, Main Division VIII of the MfS was declassified in June 2006. Neiber stated that on 24 March 1985, Major Nicholson and Sergeant Schatz followed a convoy of Soviet tanks and conducted reconnaissance of a Soviet tank range in Techentin near Ludwigslust. An East German MfS version of the events was detailed in the memorandum by Neiber and how Major Nicholson was shot and killed by a Soviet guard. Among operative measures taken by the MfS with respect to the situation was surveillance of phone calls made from Potsdam in this matter by Unit 26 of Division 5 in the Main Department VIII and collecting reactions and opinions of members of USMLM through "our agents within the USMLM".Enforced control of USMLM movements and actions within the restricted area of USMLM in Potsdam was ordered along with controls against Western mass media journalists.

Major Nicholson was awarded the Purple Heart and the Legion of Merit posthumously and was buried in the National Cemetery in Arlington. I attended the funeral along with many members and former members of our Mission. A library for the American community in Berlin was named after Major Nicholson and a building at the Defense Intelligence Agency in Washington, DC was also named after him. Although he was the only fatality suffered by our Mission, over the years many of our members were injured in crashes and deliberate rammings for which special vehicles were used by the Soviets and East Germans. Almost every officer who conducted reconnaissance tours for any length of time had shots fired at him or his car sometime. The French and British Missions also had confrontations and sustained injuries during their reconnaissance tours over the years. On 22 March 1984, L' adjutant Chef Philippe Mariotti, a member of the French military mission was killed by the Soviets.

CHAPTER 8 –
PERSPECTIVES DURING
OKINAWA AND KOREA SERVICE

THREAT ANALYSIS AT THE DEVELOPMENT CENTER

Since it was impossible for me to communicate effectively from Berlin with the Personnel Department in Washington because the Soviets intercepted all traffic, I arrived to Quantico for duty without knowing what I would be doing. It seemed to me that I had an urgent obligation to pass to the Marine Corps Schools and Development Center the new threat of Soviet weapons and tactics observed in East Germany of which most instructors and project officers were blissfully unaware. Whereas in Berlin, at the height of the Cold War the Soviet threat was real, in the Washington, DC area the Democratic Party wanted to cut the defense budget in half, forget about the communist threat and the Cold War. Democratic senators who controlled the funding for the intelligence agencies ordered the agencies to come up with estimates that there was no threat to the United States in Vietnam, Berlin, Iran or anywhere else. The Soviets were playing President Jimmy Carter like a violin and in response he essentially took the moral high ground, chastised them for human rights violations, showed them his Bible and said love thy neighbor believing the boys in the Kremlin will love you in return.

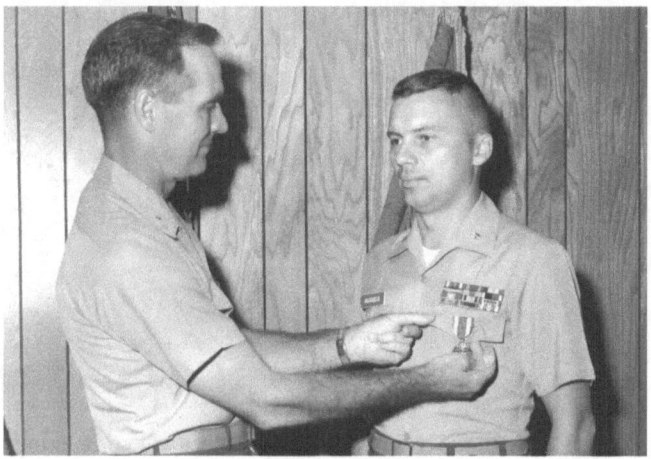

Brigadier General Noah New presenting the Meritorious Service Medal for service in East Germany, Quantico 1974.

It was a honor to be given the job of operations officer of the Amphibious Warfare Presentation Team under Colonel Jack H. Butler and Major Bill Eshelman. They helped me to rehabilitate myself from my poor health and supported me during difficult moments when I was trying to learn how to be an instructor and showman. Major Eshelman was a great inspiration and leader but I requested a transfer to the Threat Branch of the Development Center. It seemed to me that my first obligation was the presentation of the Soviet and world wide communist threat to the Marine Corps and I was not doing it under Colonel Butler. Still I helped present 21 road shows, flew 10,470 miles with the team, traveled for 55 days and had an attendance of 6,840 personnel at the shows before leaving with a heavy heart because Colonel Butler and Major Eshelman were not happy.

At the Development Center, I eventually became the head of the Threat Branch and the Foreign Science and Technology officer. During my three years with the Development Center, according to Lieutenant General J.C. Fegan's certificate of commendation which was awarded to me upon departure, I displayed superior technical knowledge and proficiency. Of particular note was my development of an effective and credible enemy-threat briefing program. This program was requested and received by commands throughout the Marine Corps as well as the United States Naval Academy and the Canadian Forces Staff College. General Fegan, added after I briefed him and his staff that through my dedication, technical expertise, and initiative, I contributed to the accomplishment of the Marine Corps Development and Education Command's mission.

Admiral Bobby R. Inman USN, presenting a certificate of completion of a Joint Armed Forces Project with representatives from Belgium, New Zealand, Iran, Saudi Arabia and Australia, Washington DC, 1977.

While at the Development Center, I was given the additional duty of threat analysis support for the Lessons Learned Study of the October 1973 Middle East War. The war only lasted about twenty days but it was characterized by a spectacular expenditure of ammunition and the employment of new Soviet weapons by the Arabs against Israel. Many of the Soviet weapons which I observed in East Germany for the first time, appeared on the battlefield in the Middle East. General P.X. Kelley, the Director of the Development Center, wanted the results of the study briefed to project officers and Fleet Marine Forces. Colonel Jerry Polakoff designated Lieutenant Colonel Con Silard and me to give the briefings and we traveled a lot for several months. I briefed the threat weapons and tactics and Lieutenant Colonel Silard briefed the lessons learned with great success and interest on the part of Marines in the Fleet Marine Forces.

In addition, using only my own unclassified photographs from East Germany, I briefed the threat to the free world of the Soviet forces and their weapons at the Marine Corps Schools. In 1977, a Basic School class liked my briefing so much that they selected me to be their instructor of the year and invited me to their graduation as a guest of honor. My briefing was well received at the Amphibious Warfare School and the Command and Staff College also. It meant a lot to me to be complimented by Major General Donald Gardner for the briefing along with many letters of appreciation from various commanding officers. Colonel Frank Manrod, who was my branch chief at first, pretty much left me alone to do my job. When Colonel James Quisenberry took over he was also supportive and an outstanding leader.

Brigadier General Stephen Olmstead presenting certificate from Lieutenant General J.C. Fegan, Quantico 1977.

RETURNING TO THE 3ᴿᴰ MARINE DIVISION ON OKINAWA

In late 1977, I was given orders to the 3rd Marine Divison on Okinawa, Japan. Shortly after I arrived, the 9th Marines needed a regimental communications officer for their deployment to Korea in Team Spirit 78 exercises and I was given the job right away after a review of my record showed that I had been a battalion communications officer with 2/9 in Vietnam. My regimental commander was Colonel Edmundson who knew me from Subic Bay. We accomplished our movement successfully to Korea despite extremely cold weather and met all our training objectives during Exercise Team Spirit – 78 with good evaluations. We were awarded the Korea Defense Service Medal for our service in Korea years later.

Upon return, Major General Adolph Schwenk, the commanding general of the 3rd Marine Division and III MAF, assigned me to the job of Assistant Chief of Staff, G-2, of the division. At 4:30 AM every morning I read all my message traffic and assigned tasks to my staff before joining at 0600AM, Major General Schwenk, Brigadier General W.H. Rice, the Chief of Staff and the Assistant Chief of Staff, G-3 in our command center for the morning briefing. After the briefing, General Schwenk would usually fly in his helicopter to visit Marines in the field or at Camp Hansen and Camp Schwab. My day started with many staff duties but then I made it a point to work with our reconnaissance, scout sniper and intelligence operations Marines over whom I had staff cognizance.

3D Marine Division General and Special Staff 31 May 1978, Camp Courtney, Okinawa, Major General Adolph Schwenk, center bottom row, with Brigadier General W. H. Rice on his right, second row, author standing between two Navy officers.

As the Assistant Chief of Staff, G-2, I had to be aware of what was going on in Korea, Taiwan, Cambodia and Vietnam. With the help of Major Don James, the Deputy G-2, and Captain Larry Burgess, officer in charge of our intelligence operations center, as well as other Marines in the G-2 section, we monitored the trouble spots. The North Koreans were sending "skunk boats" with commandos to the south and were digging tunnels under the DMZ all the time. Kim Il-Sung continued many acts of aggression and to starve, torture and mass murder people in the tradition of his mentor Joseph Stalin. While doing that he kidnapped blonde women from Sweden for sex and bought many Mercedes Benz cars from Germany for his collection.

In Taiwan, President Carter and the Democratic Party did all they could to roll back our support for our staunch anti-communist ally. It seemed that the Carter administration wanted to give everything to the communists like the Roosevelt administration had done before. Thanks to Major General John Singlaub, US Army, who fought against the Carter plan to abandon South Korea, President Carter succeeded in only withdrawing one battalion of the 2nd Infantry Division from Seoul.

In Vietnam, the Democrats continued to reduce our support for Saigon until it finally fell on 30 April 1975. The North Vietnamese then shunted 400,000 South Vietnamese civil servants, doctors, lawyers, teachers, military officers and intellectuals into Soviet style "reeducation" camps. Like in Stalin's Gulag, the inmates in the about forty concentration camps in South Vietnam suffered from malnutrition, diseases and torture while reports of summary executions abounded. At a large camp near the town of Tan Hiep, south of Saigon, many prisoners were beaten and shackled in the sun without water. In other camps, prisoners were locked in the same "tiger cages" which aroused protests in America during the war when the Saigon government used them but when Hanoi used them there was no complaint from the same American protesters and our news media. The camps were denounced by Amnesty International which monitors human rights violations. Amnesty International also denounced the murder of two million Cambodians by the Chinese communist supported Pol Pot regime and the Khmer Rouge.

According to an editor of the Wall Street Journal, who spoke at his retirement ceremony with Secretary Henry Kissinger in attendance, we lost the war in Vietnam because of a two-bit burglary in the Watergate apartment building and partisan politics. In 1975, the Soviet Pacific fleet arrived in Vietnam and the Soviet armed forces took over our multi-million dollar facilities and equipment. The communists in Hanoi enslaved the South Vietnamese people without any protests from American activists and used the gulag camps to discard the skilled people needed for national recovery. The torture and mass murder of free people in the Republic of Vietnam by the communists caused the flight of one million refugees by boat many of whom came to America. Although as a Marine officer, it was incumbent upon me to stay clear of politics, I could not help but read the reports we were getting with sadness and felt that we needed someone like President Ronald Reagan to come to the rescue and in the White House.

SERVICE WITH THE 9TH MARINE AMPHIBIOUS BRIGADE

During late 1978, it was an honor to be assigned to the 9th Marine Amphibious Brigade (MAB) as the Assistant Chief of Staff, G-2, because the brigade was commanded by Brigadier General W.H. Rice, the Chief of Staff was Colonel Frank Petersen and the brigade was the 911 emergency reaction force from Major General Schwenk's III MAF. The III MAF was made up of the 3rd Marine Division and the 1st Marine Aircraft Wing and guarded the outposts of freedom in the Pacific and Indian Ocean areas. If someone was attacked by the communists and the Marines were sent to help, the 9th MAB was most ready and would go within hours as the lead element for our support to who ever was fighting for their freedom. During my tour of duty, the most likely place to be attacked by communists was South Korea. We kept our plans current to go to Korea on a moment's notice to help General Vessey and the US Army 2nd Infantry Division if need be.

Joint Exercise, Pohang, Korea 1978.

During Joint Exercises Brigadier General W. H. Rice being briefed with author standing nearby, Pohang, Korea 1978.

In order to be ready to help General Vessey in Seoul, General Rice, Lieutenant Colonel Knudsen our G-3, I as the G-2, Captain David Mize our G-1 and Lieutenant Colonel Burt Deckel our headquarters commandant flew from Okinawa to Korea for command post and joint US-Korean exercises. We also conducted a command post exercise (CPX) from the USS Blue Ridge. During the end of the CPX, a typhoon caused the Blue Ridge captain to move the ship first into the eye of the typhoon where the water was completely still and then into Hong Kong for shelter from the severe weather. While in Hong Kong we were allowed ashore and enjoyed the liberty a great deal.

During one staff visit to Korea, we observed the ongoing shootings and threats from the communists at the DMZ and the required readiness of the US and Korean forces. We coordinated and tested our plans with the Korean Marines and got to know our counterparts. One evening the Korean Marines held a dinner party in General Rice's honor to which I was also invited. The Korean Marines were highly professional and dedicated to defend their country against any attack from the North.

SERVING IN THE PLANS AND ESTIMATES BRANCH AS A REGIONAL ANALYST

In February 1979, after service with the 9th Marine Amphibious Brigade, I was assigned the duties of regional analyst at the Plans and Estimates Branch, Headquarters, US Marine Corps, Washington, DC. Since I just came from Okinawa, it made sense to make me responsible for plans and estimates about Korea, China, Vietnam and the Soviet Union's Pacific Ocean area forces. During my first few days on the job, we had a record setting snow-storm which buried us in several feet of snow. All non-essential personnel were told to stay home because of the snow. I thought that I was non-essential until I got a phone call from a duty officer ordering me to come to work right away and to look at message traffic in the Pentagon command center.

To come to the Pentagon command center was difficult since only a few lanes had been cleared of snow on two roads and there was only parking for about twenty cars at the river entrance. I parked my car and found all doors locked except one leading to the command center where I picked up my messages. After returning to my car, I found a $150.00 parking ticket which I paid to Alexandria by check and discovered that the People's Republic of China had launched an attack against the People's Republic of Vietnam with five armies. I took the messages to Colonel John Donahue who told me that we would have to brief General Louis H. Wilson, the Commandant of the Marine Corps. Apparently, the Hanoi leaders believed in the "Domino Theory" after the U.S. was forced out and wanted to take over all of Indo-China but the Chinese stopped the Hanoi expansion at the cost of 50,000 KIA and bailed us out. General Wilson found the briefing interesting but we all agreed that no action was required by Marines and that the war would be probably resolved in due time between Hanoi and Beijing.

Brigadier General Clyde Dean presenting a Certificate of Commendation, Headquarters 1980. The uniform of the day was civilian attire often at work.

The rest of my service as a regional analyst was less exciting. After Colonel Donahue retired, I served under Brigadier General Clyde Dean who gave me a certificate of commendation for my expertise and professional knowledge, particularly with regard to Soviet weaponry, tactics and doctrine, which coupled with hard work and keen analytical ability produced excellent results. He added that short notice and scheduled briefings by me enabled headquarters principals to be totally abreast of current events as well as future projections. Since I had served with General Dean in Vietnam and greatly respected his service it meant a lot to get the certificate from him. He later was promoted to Lieutenant General and retired as the Chief of Staff at Marine Corps headquarters.

The work of planning and estimating in the Pentagon was done in a systematic way with color codes for each action level. My input was at the basic level where most of the work was done and required going to inter-service meetings. Prior to the meetings it was necessary to do research, to know the subject matter and the Marine Corps position as papers were gone through line by line. To be more effective, I signed up for the Naval War College off-campus seminar program given in the Pentagon and I took night courses at Georgetown University in international relations. General Dean provided help and guidance to action officers through his branch chiefs and operations officer. Sometimes staff officers would call me with questions about the region for which I was responsible. One question which was asked of me sometimes with a touch of humor was which was the best Chinese restaurant in our area. My answer was that it was secret information only given to special persons and the best Chinese restaurant was Eddie L. K. Tsui's & Lily Tsui's Peking Gourmet Inn on Leesburg Pike, Falls Church, Virginia.

ASSIGNMENT TO THE NAVY STAFF AS AN ACTION OFFICER

In mid-1980, a Marine officer was needed on the Navy Staff to work on issues pertaining to Korea and I was selected for the job. At first I did not realize that it was quite an honor to be on the staff of the Chief of Naval Operations who was Admiral Thomas Hayward. Then while first working for Rear Admiral Shapiro and then Rear Admiral Butz, it became clear that as an action officer I was contributing to the work of Navy officers who were making important decisions involving personnel and equipment. President Ronald Reagan had just been elected and turned around the self-defeating policies which got President Carter kicked out of office. Secretary John Lehman started to rebuild the badly depleted Navy and amphibious ships needed for Marines were also included in the upgrade.

While taking Naval War College classes, I had to read the famous history of the Greek wars by Thucydides entitled *The Pelopennesian War*. The book was recommended to the Naval War College by Henry Kissinger because the democrats in Athens behaved during their war with Sparta like the democrats in Washington, DC did during the Vietnam war and both lost their war. From reading other sources, it became clear to me that the Vietnam war was about the Cold War and not Vietnam. When President Reagan took over from President Carter the communists were advancing everywhere in the world while the democrats had spent all the tax payer money on left wing social issues. The communists were spending their money on pushing the US and the free world out of Vietnam, Nicaragua, Grenada, Afghanistan, Hong Kong, Panama and other places and the democrats in America were spending our money on culture wars, abortion, welfare, drug addicts, the destruction of law enforcement, the elimination of family values and marriage. Freedom fighters in foreign countries were being abandoned by us under laws like the Congressman Bohlen amendment and communists like the Sandinistas where openly supported by the Black Caucus in Congress along with liberals in New York and Hollywood.

With regard to Hollywood, communist intelligence services made the elite in Los Angeles one of their top priority targets. Through communist organizations in New York and on college campuses, foreign agents from Havana, Hanoi, Beijing and Moscow were sending propaganda about what Hollywood could do to advance the causes of world socialism and communist solidarity. The Communist guidance was also willingly propagated by news media moguls and reporters. Some Hollywood personalities even took it upon themselves to find out what the communists wanted so that they could serve our enemies better. Although the communists got no help from Elia Kazan, Charlton Heston, Ronald Reagan, and some others, the vast majority of Hollywood producers and actors were glad to push the communist party line in many movies. Movies about Vietnam were made which depicted Americans as bad, on drugs, mentally unbalanced and killing innocent people.

After watching several such movies, I felt that there was not a single shred of truth in them and that the producers put everything bad that ever happened in the world in their movies about Vietnam. The Communists were usually depicted as the innocent victims and idealists saving the oppressed, while Americans were the bad guys. The Communist intelligence services could never have done for themselves what the Hollywood and New York elite did for their propaganda efforts against the American people. It took many years until in 2002, a movie with Mel Gibson entitled, "We Were Soldiers Once" finally showed more factually the service of our soldiers and their families in Vietnam.

During mid-1981, the Cold War appeared to be going in favor of the communists and the Reagan administration had its hands full to pick up the pieces after all the set-backs under President Carter. After working on the Korea issues as an action officer, an estimate paper was completed by my branch chief and passed review by Admiral Shapiro. We were then invited to the executive building near the White House for a meeting with Admiral Bobby R. Inman who wanted to go over the paper carefully. We entered the conference room and waited with our notes and background materials for Admiral Inman. I was ready to defend our thesis that Kim Il-Sung and his Stalinist regime were a threat to peace and were starving millions of Koreans. When Admiral Inman arrived he was a little angry with Admiral Shapiro for bringing action officers, me and two Navy officers, to the meeting and told us to wait outside. We heard later that Admiral Shapiro pointed out to Admiral Inman that we the action officers had written the estimate, knew the facts and should not have been asked to leave. We drank coffee outside and all went well. The estimate was approved, published by the Defense Department and used for planning. It was one of my last projects before getting orders to become the Defense Attaché in the Dominican Republic.

Admiral Thomas Hayward, Chief of Naval Operations,
Pentagon, 1982.

To Colonel Dominick Nargele,
    With high regard for your proven
professional competence and loyal
dedication to our great Navy—Marine
Corps team.

                    Admiral Thomas H Hayward
                    Chief of Naval Operations

CHAPTER 9 –
THE WARS IN THE DOMINICAN REPUBLIC

After several months of Spanish language training, on 1 June 1982, I replaced Colonel Jaime Sabater as the Defense Attaché in Santo Domingo. Colonel Sabater informed me that I was also the Naval Attaché and the Naval Attaché for Air. Our Army Attaché was Lieutenant Colonel Larry Biddel. Our Air Attaché was Colonel Samuel Grow but he was stationed in Caracas, Venezuela and only came to Santo Domingo with his aircraft once or twice a year.

During the early 1970s, our full time Air Attaché was kidnapped by communists and tortured. After he was released by the communists he was in such poor health that he died six months later. The US Air Force never replaced him and gave the Air Attaché job in Santo Domingo to Colonel Grow in Caracas as an additional duty.

The embassy was running smoothly under Ambassador Yost when I arrived until Ambassador Robert Anderson took over. Ambassador Anderson was a foreign service officer and came from Massachusetts. He believed in leadership by overbearing control and removal of personnel from office with career ending performance evaluations. Upon arrival, Ambassador Anderson first fired the Deputy Director of the Agency for International Development. Next to go was the Agricultural Attaché followed by the Economic Counselor. After that, the ambassador attacked and fired his Administrative Officer over the color of the new ambassador's car and other similar issues. One secretary got a transfer immediately while others suffered for as long as they could until they ran out screaming for help. The large swimming pool and tennis courts in the embassy which were open to embassy personnel and their families under Ambassador Yost were placed off limits by Ambassador Anderson and reserved only for himself and his wife. Ambassador Anderson thought that when he was called "Tip" by his staff, that it was an honored reference to his mentor, Congressman Tip O'Neil of Massachusetts. In reality, the staff made up the name "Tip" to stand for "Turkey In Paradise".

Ambassador Anderson came to Santo Domingo from Norfolk, Virginia, where he had been the Political Advisor (PolAd) to Admiral Harry Train, Commander in Chief Atlantic (CinCLant). I was told by Navy officers during ship visits that Ambassador Anderson was disliked by everybody in Norfolk but Admiral Train gave the ambassador a pass on the performance appraisal because he wanted to avoid trouble and controversy. When Captain Leighton "Snuffy" Smith came with a large ship, the USS Kalamazoo, on a visit to Santo Domingo, I had to meet him by myself without the ambassador. After I told Captain Smith that Ambassador Anderson could not come to welcome him, the captain said that is good because I do not want to speak to him anyway and my admiral in Norfolk sends a message to the ambassador which is: "Stick it in your ear!".

Despite the ambassador's leadership style, my tour of duty was interesting and enjoyable. Only after one month in Santo Domingo, President Antonio Guzman who lost his bid for reelection to a member of his own party, committed suicide in the presidential palace. Before shooting himself in the head, at 0200 on 4 July 1982, President Guzman reportedly had the top military leaders kneel before him and swear that they would not try to overthrow the government. After President Guzman shot himself he was still alive for a while and I conducted a rescue operation to get him to Miami for surgery. I called Roosevelt Roads, Puerto Rico, and they launched a C-12 passenger jet immediately to pick up President Guzman. President Guzman died before the aircraft reached Santo Domingo and I turned it around with many thanks. At the same time, we first checked and then rechecked many times the main military installations and observed that the service chiefs remained true to their oath with no military units moving anywhere to overthrow the government.

After President Guzman mortally wounded himself in Santo Domingo, a concern existed in the diplomatic community there and in the embassy that the armed forces might suddenly take over the government instead of allowing the constitutional process to take its course. This concern was heightened since the new President-elect Salvador Jorge Blanco was a leftist who had served as an official with the anti-US forces during the 1965 Civil War and was considered to be a threat to freedom by some senior officers in the rightist pro-US armed forces. After helping the ambassador in getting emergency teams from Puerto Rico and another from Texas airborne, in an attempt to keep the wounded President alive, I then continuously deployed the resources of my office to monitor the situation for several days and correctly assess the posture of the armed forces. This resulted in accurate reporting and crisis supervision which was commended by Lieutenant General James A. Williams, USA, the director of the Defense Intelligence Agency, in a message to me. Detailed surveillance of subsequent events insured the constitutional process could run its course with the Vice President taking over the reigns of government for forty days until the President-elect was sworn in.

During the crisis after the presidential suicide, my office and I supported the constitutional process, democracy and freedom for the Dominican people as I learned to do in the Pentagon, at the Naval War College and Georgetown University. There was little guidance or information about how to deal with the situation from the ambassador and I assumed we were on the right course. Then I started to get reports about the leftist Dominican Revolutionary Party in power and what the plans were of the new president. The plans were to retire or fire all pro-American members of the armed forces who had fought on our side during the civil war of 1965 and replace them with communists who had fought against us.

The Carter administration supported with tax-payer money the left-wing government of Guzman against pro-US civilian and military leaders as requested by Communist activists in the Democratic Party in America. President Salvador Jorge Blanco was expecting to continue to benefit from the previously sanctioned anti-American activities. There was only one problem. President Ronald Reagan got inaugurated in 1981 and he did not like supporting communists and our enemies. To this day, even in retirement the media often report President Carter as still supporting Fidel Castro and other left-wing leaders in the region. Reportedly, when the election of left-wing President Hugo Chavez was disputed in Venezuela, President Carter certified the allegedly questionable victory within hours. Since then, Chavez said the worst things possible about President Bush and the United States of America. Chavez has made every effort to hurt American interests and to endanger our country.

In order to understand how we got to the point of firing pro-US military leaders, I had to hear and learn about the past. While at the Marine Corps Schools in Quantico, I heard a lot about Marines who had served in the Dominican Republic during the US occupation of 1916 to 1924 and now I could see for myself what they were talking about. According to Brigadier General E. H. Simmons, the history of the country was marked by much turbulence and unrest. The Dominican Republic gained its independence from Haiti in 1844 and had alternated between dictatorships and less restrictive governments. There were 26 different constitutions until under the US Marine occupation of 1916 to 1924 a stable government was created with law and order. After the Marines left, a liberal democratic government ran the country but it was weak and corrupt. In 1930, a US Marine trained guardia national sergeant, Rafael Leonidas Trujillo, took over and ran the country like a Marine rifle platoon until he was assassinated on 30 May 1961. He promoted himself to general during his rule and like many dictators of the 1930s in Europe, at first he did many good things for his people and country.

As General Trujillo's power increased, there were more and more abuses by his family members which got him into trouble at home and there was growing animosity from his Caribbean neighbors. It was explained to me that his children and relatives were getting into trouble and he would have to bail them out while the leaders in neighboring countries were increasingly plotting against him. Trujillo considered his main enemies to be Castro of Cuba, Betancourt of Venezuela and Munoz Marin of Puerto Rico.

According to General Simmons, during 1960, the Organization of American States censured Trujillo for aiding an assassination attempt against Betancourt. However, Betancourt had been involved a year before in a Cuba-based invasion of the Dominican Republic. On 14 June 1959, 45 guerrillas were air landed at Constanza, a mountain resort, and 145 guerrillas landed by boat on the coast west of Puerto Plata against Trujillo. The invaders had been a mixture of Cubans, Guatemalans, Dominican exiles and several American communists. After ten days of operations, the Dominican armed forces crushed the invasion, killing most of the invaders and capturing several prisoners.

The Dominican Army consisted of about 20,000 soldiers in six brigades at my time there. The brigades were stationed in six regional zones of responsibility in the country. The company was the basic combat and administrative unit. In most towns, there was a well constructed small fort (fortaleza) in which one company was stationed. The Dominican Air Force consisted of about 10,000 personnel with about 160 aircraft. The main air base was at San Isidro. The air force also had a northern base at Santiago and a southern base at Barahona.

The Dominican Navy consisted of about 8,000 personnel and had two destroyers, two frigates, five corvettes, twenty patrol boats, two presidential yachts and various support craft. The main naval base was at Santo Domingo but units were stationed in various ports through out the country for border patrol and coastal security duties. In addition, the National Police with 7,000 members had to be considered one of the armed forces since they were organized like the army and had heavy infantry weapons and armored personnel carriers. Finally, the most feared organization was the military intelligence service with about five thousand members and many paid and unpaid informants.

THE TRUJILLO ERA ENDING

At about 10:15PM on 30 May 1961, the Trujillo era should have ended when he was assassinated by thirteen men who ambushed him on the coastal highway on the way from Santo Domingo to San Cristobal to see his mistress.

However, his older son, General Rafael Trujillo, better known as Ramfis, who reportedly played around with Zsa Zsa Gabor and Kim Novak, took over as the head of the armed forces and revenged the death of his father by hundreds of arrests, the torture and execution of dozens of people. As the head of the armed forces, Ramfis was the real leader of the country and President Joaquin Balaguer was only useful in making speeches but had no real power.

For a time, it looked like Ramfis might lead his country toward a more democratic form of government as he liquidated about $800 million of Trujillo's financial empire. Subsequent actions by Ramfis, however, indicated that there was no basis for liberalization and movement towards democracy. Since the US embassy members could not work with Ramfis and he could become an even more radical right or left-wing leader, it was decided to offer him a golden parachute backed up by a US naval air and sea power demonstration.

A replacement was found for Ramfis by the US Naval Attache, Lieutenant Colonel Edwin H. Simmons, USMC, in Brigadier General Rafael Rodriguez Echavarria, a rated pilot and commander of the air base at Barahona. General Echavarria and President Balaguer handled the resignation and departure of Ramfis well but their popularity did not last long. Three parties opposed the Balaguer government. First, the National Civic Union (UCN) was headed by Dr. Viriato Fiallo and was the largest party. Second, the Dominican Revolutionary Party (PRD) headed by Juan Bosch was the next strongest. Last, the "14th of June" party was the farthest to the left, named after the 14 June 1959 invasion against Trujillo, and although it was not quite hard line communist it was anti-US and pro-Castro. The three parties forced Balaguer out of office.

After a period of civil unrest and instability, Juan Bosch was elected president by defeating Viriato Fiallo of the UCN. I met the sister of President Bosch and she talked about her famous brother many years later to me. Bosch did not do well and almost started a war with Haiti when he was overthrown by Brigadier General Elias Wessin y Wessin with the support of the armed forces and conservative political leaders. In December 1963, President Lyndon B. Johnson recognized the military imposed government providing national elections would be held in 1965.

THE US INTERVENTION IN THE DOMINICAN REPUBLIC

In order to make sense of subsequent developments I had to understand the events of 1965. After President Johnson recognized the new right of center government, Donald Reid Cabral emerged as the leader and was in office until early in 1965 when at least two separate groups, one conservative and the other Bosch's left-wing PRD, were planning coups. On Saturday, 24 April 1965, angry left-wing demonstrators took to the streets demanding that Juan Bosch be re-installed and rebellious soldiers passed out thousands of guns to the demonstrators. The police, loyal to Reid Cabral, restored order but about 1,200 soldiers from the "16th of August" fortaleza outside of Santo Domingo continued the "rebellion". Then Reid Cabral asked Lieutenant Colonel Ralph Heywood, USMC, the Naval Attaché at the time, who was on a hunting trip with Brigadier General Antonio Imbert Barreras, one of two surviving Trujillo assassins, if the US would intervene to save the government from the left-wing rebellion. The US took the request seriously and many years later, I talked to Reid Cabral and Imbert Barreras about what happened next.

On 24 April 1965, the 6th Marine Expeditionary Unit (MEU) embarked in the ships of the Ready Amphibious Task Group, was notified that a communist-inspired coup was threatening the Dominican government. The ready group then moved to Haina, a sugar port west of Santo Domingo and prepared to evacuate about 1,200 US citizens. On 25 April, the rebels took control of downtown Santo Domingo and rumors were ciculating that Juan Bosch was about to take over. On 26 April, General Wessin y Wessin asked for US intervention and Washington approved the evacuation of US citizens.

The evacuation began at 1300 on 27 April by truck and bus to Haina where Navy ships were waiting. Then rebels fired with machine guns over the heads of the people waiting to be evacuated overland and US Marine helicopters came in and flew out 1,712 persons. The same day, attempts by General Wessin y Wessin to negotiate a ceasefire failed and he sent his loyal troops into the city supported by the Dominican Air Force. Hundreds of people were killed and many more were wounded as Bosch's PRD party lost control of the mob and Castro supported activists along with armed Cuban agents.

On Wednesday, 28 April, the streets of Santo Domingo were filled with demonstrators and activists which were out of control. According to Brigadier General E. H. Simmons, one platoon of Marines from 3rd Battalion, 6th Marines (3/6), was flown to protect the US embassy and another platoon was flown to the evacuation site where civilians were still arriving to be flown out by Marine helicopters. At 6:00PM, President Johnson authorized the landing of 500 Marines and the headquarters of 3/6 along with two rifle companies arrived at the landing zone near the Embajador Hotel. That evening 684 civilians were flown out and the following day 516 more were helolifted out by Marine helicopters. By nightfall all of 3/6 totaling 1,500 Marines landed and took control of their area of responsibility.

At 2:30AM on 30 April, the 3rd Brigade, 82nd Airborne Division, began landing in C-130s at the San Isidro air force base. Lieutenant Colonel Doug

Guiler US Army, was on the fourth C-130 to land and told me about it later. Marine Battalion Landing Team (BLT) 1/6 was also airlifted into San Isidro and Brigadier General John H. Bouker, Commanding General, 4th Marine Expeditionary Brigade arrived there with his staff. Later, BLT 1/8 arrived at San Isidro and BLT 1/2 arrived offshore on board the LPH Okinawa to serve as a floating reserve. The Marines of 3/6 moved east and the paratroopers moved west to link up and get the uprising under control. Then Brigadier General Antonio Imbert Barreras, Dominican Army, took over the loyal troops in the San Isidro area and began the cleanup of fragmented rebel groups in the old part of Santo Domingo. When I talked to Imbert Barreras, about his historic role, many years later, he was the only living Trujillo assassin and had been promoted to Lieutenant General by President Salvador Jorge Blanco.

The S-3 of the 6th MEU at the time was Major Stephen Olmstead, who stated many years later as a retired Lieutenant General, that a Joint Evacuation Exercise with the 3rd Brigade, 82nd Airborne Division had been conducted at Vieques, three weeks before the landings at Santo Domingo. The S-3 of the 3rd Brigade, was Major Philip Kaplan, who was General Olmstead's classmate at the Infantry School, Fort Benning Georgia, also a next door neighbor and retired as a Major General. The 3rd Brigade returned to the Continental U.S. after the joint exercise in Vieques only to fly back on 30 April for the landings at San Isidro in the Dominican Republic.

The uprising never spread beyond downtown Santo Domingo and the rest of the country remained quiet. The bulk of the Dominican armed forces stayed out of the struggle. As the Marines and paratroopers rapidly reestablished government control the casualties were counted and consisted of about 300 Dominicans killed and about 2,000 wounded. With three Marine battalion landing teams ashore and one afloat, about 8,000 Marines were involved in the operation. Marines sustained 9 KIA and 30 WIA, about one-third of the total American casualties.

It seems to me that clearly the arrival of the Marines and the 82nd Airborne, displayed President Johnson's resolve to prevent another pro-left regime from taking power in the Caribbean. President Johnson did not want communist agents within the rebel movement to create "another Cuba" he said. On 31 August, the left-wing Constitutionalists and right of center Loyalists signed an OAS proposed agreement of reconciliation. The agreement established an interim government under Hector Garcia-Godoy pending elections the following June. During the interim period, the Dominican armed forces were reunited and many rebel officers were exiled or given overseas assignments. Public utilities and services were restored and economic recovery was started.

ELECTION OF PRESIDENT JOAQUIN BALAGUER

On 6 May 1965, the OAS voted to create an Inter-American Peace Force for the civil strife in Santo Domingo. On 25 May, the lead elements of a Brazilian infantry battalion arrived and on the next day the Marines started to withdraw. By 6 June, the Marines had departed and as far as the Marine Corps was concerned the Dominican intervention was over. In just a few weeks, the Marines and the 82nd Airborne had accomplished their mission, stopped the Dominican civil war, separated rebels from Loyalists, forced a military stalemate and ended most of the fighting. The US forces had achieved President Johnson's main objective of preventing the establishment of another Castro-style regime in the Americas and the loss of the Dominican Republic to communism.

According to Major L. M. Greenberg of the Center of Military History, Lieutenant General Bruce Palmer, the US Army ground force commander, strengthened positions in Santo Domingo and prepared a cadre headquarters with an administrative foundation for the Inter-American Peace Force. With the line of communication established by Marines and paratroopers separating Loyalists and rebels, General Palmer stressed restraint and neutrality. During the next four months, US soldiers guaranteed relative peace and pressured the Dominican factions to come to terms. In mid-May, 1,600 Latin soldiers and policemen from Brazil, Honduras, Paraguay, Nicaragua, El Salvador and Costa Rica arrived and assumed peace keeping duties. Then US soldiers started to depart until only 6,243 men were left by late 1965. On 27 September 1966, the last US soldier departed and the OAS deactivated its peace force. The casualty totals in the end were 27 US KIA, 172 US WIA and 17 OAS peace force WIA. Total Dominican casualties were about 300 KIA and about 1,700 WIA. As a footnote, it seemed interesting to me, that my Chief of Mission in Potsdam, Colonel Frederick C. Turner USA, had served in Santo Domingo as the Secretary of the Staff of the Inter-American Peace Force, commanded first by Brazilian Lieutenant General Alzim and subsequently by Brazilian Lieutenant General Braga.

The good news for President Johnson was that he restored peace and brought democracy to the Dominican people for many decades to come. The bad news was that communists in Latin America, in the US and in our Congress, attacked President Johnson for his unannounced and unilateral action. Deep cleavages between the President and Congress were opened in matters of foreign policy, as he had to contend with spoiled baby boom children, who had been co-opted by the Soviet Union's propaganda moles, in the left-wing of the Democratic Party. Ideological debates continued long after the Marines and paratroopers left and eventually encompassed President

Johnson's desire to support democracy in Vietnam against the communists who could slaughter people with impunity and do no wrong as far as many members of the US Congress, academia and media were concerned. Somehow it became popular in the US by doves and liberals to criticize President Johnson for restoring peace and to give tacit support to communists around the world.

There was more good news in the Dominican Republic for President Johnson when in June 1966, under the watchful eyes of three sets of international observers, Joaquin Balaguer was elected president. The elections were honest and peaceful. Balaguer, the former president under Trujillo, representing political moderates, defeated Juan Bosch and won with over 57 percent of the vote. General Wessin y Wessin was removed from the Dominican Army and named the Dominican Counsel General to the US in Washington. At the same time, the Constitutionalist military leader who directed the left-wing rebels in the civil war, Colonel Francisco Caamano was named the Dominican military attache to Great Britain and flown to London.

In 1973, Colonel Caamano was killed by Dominican soldiers while attempting to return to the Dominican Republic secretly with a small band of conspirators from Cuba. During my tour of duty, the death of Caamano became a communist saga widely published in Latin America and the US. While I was serving as Defense Attaché, I was often offered literature about Caamano which was paid for by Castro and US donations. I respectfully declined and once told a visitor that the Dominican soldiers who killed Caamano were still using US Marine Corps manuals for their training and were defending their country against communist invaders in the finest tradition of the US Marines. During my tour of duty, I was invited often to Dominican army parades and was impressed by the precision and professionalism of the Dominicans. They followed the Landing Party Manual closely and drilled just like US Marines.

BALAGUER SERVED UNTIL THE CARTER ADMINISTRATION TOOK OVER IN WASHINGTON

After President Balaguer was elected in 1966, he served successfully for three terms with the support of the moderates in the Dominican Republic. Three US presidents, Johnson, Nixon and Ford, also supported Balaguer. After the two-bit robbery at the Watergate apartment building, Democrats in the US assaulted the White House until in 1977, Jimmy Carter was elected president. President Carter, the Democrats said, was needed with the bible which he carried at the Naval Academy all the time to wash away the sins of those who fought against communism in the Cold War in the Dominican

Republic and defended the outposts of freedom around the world. President Carter brought self-righteous indignation against freedom fighters in Vietnam, Korea, Germany and the Dominican Republic.

One year after the Carter administration came to power, the left-wing PRD party ousted Balaguer in the Dominican Republic and President Antonio Guzman became president. Everything that the US and the OAS force fought for during the Civil War of 1965 was abandoned to the communists under President Carter. Castro found a friend in the White House and a wave of communist aggression in Latin America was launched with the power of President Carter's bible and US Democrats behind it.

When I arrived in Santo Domingo in June 1982, the Carter administration had influenced the swing of the pendulum to the left for four years and another PRD president, Salvador Jorge Blanco, was carried into office by Carter's momentum for another four years. Although President Reagan was inaugurated in 1981, the left-wing presidency of Salvador Jorge Blanco was just getting started for another four-year term. Without much political training, I did not understand the forces unleashed in Santo Domingo by President Carter which were making my life difficult.

Ambassador Anderson explained nothing to me and Brigadier General Donald Goodman, USAF, my reporting senior and head of attaches had no idea about what was happening. Every day something negative was reported to me by friends and sources in Santo Domingo. My personal observations confirmed the bad news and when I double checked the cause usually was the left-wing PRD party and President Salvador Jorge Blanco's administration. First, I heard from the American Chamber of Commerce that PRD appointed inspectors were delaying US imported goods on the loading docks to get even with the US for the Dominican intervention. Meat and other food products from the US were being deliberately left to rot on the piers by the inspectors because it was called capitalist produce and therefore unwelcome.

Second, a Dominican admiral who was the assistant secretary of state of the armed forces and graciously accepted an invitation to my house for lunch was fired for doing that by President Salvador Jorge Blanco the next day. How did President Salvador Jorge Blanco know about the lunch? The answer was that all servants, drivers, gardeners and administrative personnel hired by the embassy were agents of the Dominican intelligence service who reported on my every move. There was little or no security in the embassy and the ambassador was not concerned.

Third, Castro who was blessed and absolved of his sins by the Carter administration was increasingly influential. Castro delivered free communist propaganda textbooks to all schools describing the US as the source of all evil. The university in Santo Domingo was covered with pro-Castro and anti-US slogans. Also, he forced moderate businessmen into bankruptcy so that they would not be able to support Balaguer. For example, Cuban agents bribed officials to buy commercial fertilizer from their plant in Panama at reduced cost until the plant of a Dominican businessman was forced into bankruptcy Then the Cubans raised the price of their fertilizer making more money and celebrated having destroyed the private property of the businessman who was anti-communist and anti-Castro. When the businessman asked for help from Ambassador Anderson he got none and in desperation came to my office for help asking me as the Defense Attaché to do something. When I reported problems like that to Washington, Ambassador Anderson was not happy. He called General Goodman and complained that I was a trouble maker to him and the U.S. State Department.

Last, there were reports of sporadic violence against Dominicans by communist gunmen throughout the country which was never reported by the embassy. Colonel Sabater sold me his .22 caliber automatic for $90.00 and I carried it in my back pocket when I wore my uniform in public. To the communists the Marine uniform which I was wearing every day was a walking target. When I tried to explain the situation to Ambassador Anderson he got angry and told everyone in the embassy, including military assistance and drug enforcement agency personnel who were often in danger that they could not "carry a gun". The order was to go out and meet some of the bad guys unarmed just like at first in Vietnam. Many years later, Major General W. H. Rice, USMC (Ret), mentioned to me, that while commanding the 2nd Force Reconnaissance Company, one of his platoons was also instructed not to carry weapons during reconnaissance operations, by a US Ambassador.

After much soul searching and discussion with other embassy personnel, who were walking targets everyday, I decided to obey the ambassador's order not to carry "a gun" by carrying "two guns". I carried my concealed .45 caliber pistol along with the .22 caliber automatic all the time. Dominican military officers had urged me to do that from the day I arrived saying it was too dangerous to be unarmed while in uniform. When I informed General Goodman of the situation, I received no reply and was described as a troublemaker by some in the attache affairs office in the Pentagon.

INAUGURATION OF PRESIDENT SALVADOR JORGE BLANCO, RECEPTIONS AND SERVING WITH THE COUNTRY TEAM

In August 1982, Salvador Jorge Blanco was inaugurated as president and Ambassador Ellsworth Bunker led the US delegation which included Ambassador William Middendorf, members of the Reagan administration and Congress. I met Congressman Charles Rangel, (D-NY) whom I liked as a person but did not like his politics and escorted Ambassador Middendorf while he attended the ceremonies. Shortly afterwards, I was invited by the air force to ceremonies for the President at San Isidro and he spoke to many but ignored me completely. It appeared to me that since Marines were on the side of the Loyalists during the 1965 Civil War and he was a constitutionalist rebel official he did not seem to want to speak to me or shake my hand. In 1982, the PRD, party of the president, gained a majority in both houses of Congress but the economy was ailing badly. The PRD then began to implement economic adjustment and recovery policies based on an austerity program with the cooperation of the International Monetary Fund (IMF).

Greeting the US Delegation for the Presidential Inauguration in Santo Domingo, August 1982, *Mrs. Ellsworth Bunker, Congressman and Mrs. Mickey Edwards, (R-OK) and Ambassador William Middendorf are visible in the photograph.*

One of my duties as Defense Attaché was to entertain Dominican military leaders in my house. During the first large function for over one hundred guests, the power cable broke in front of my house. Generals and admirals with their wives had to step over a live wire cable at first but the Chief of National Police became very angry at the power company and got them to come right away. I learned during the functions at my house that all officers had guns with them and their aides were armed also. In addition, service chiefs had armed security personnel and armored vehicles with them at all times. When asking for permission to carry a gun like everybody else in uniform, in view of the kidnapping of our air attaché, the ambassador said no and General Goodman did nothing. As an officer of the armed forces it did not seem to make much sense to be unarmed in the environment which existed at the time in Santo Domingo.

Congressman Charles Rangel (D-NY) and Political Officer Cletis Mitchler at embassy reception, Santo Domingo, August 1982.

During my entire tour, I participated in daily morning meetings as a member of the Country Team. When ever possible, I kept the ambassador, the deputy chief of mission (DCM) and the staff advised on military matters which had political impact. With the additional duty as Naval Attache, I coordinated with the help of my office staff, all aspects of ship visits, including the visit by Admiral Wesley McDonald, CINCLANT with the USS Nashville in March of 1983. Successful visits during which I was commended included ones by the USS O'Bannon, the USS Kalamazoo and the USS Mahan, in addition to the CINCLANT visit.

In June 1982, upon completing the Naval War College, I was selected an honor graduate and had to fly to Newport from Santo Domingo to my graduation where Secretary of Defense Casper Weinberger presented me with a trophy. My office obtained diplomatic clearances for all visiting aircraft and ships. In a number of cases rapid action was taken in behalf of US aircrews when they experienced equipment problems or required emergency refueling.

SECURITY QUESTIONS, HAND GRENADE INCIDENT AND OFFICER'S LUNCH

My house in Santo Domingo was rented through the embassy and beautiful for entertaining but it was infested with rats and mosquitoes which I could not eliminate. The house was guarded by an armed sentry provided by the Dominican Navy. Two maids and a gardner provided by the embassy kept the place up. The two drivers in my office also served as bar tenders during social functions. What ever guests said to me or to anyone else was reported by the staff immediately to the Dominican security service. As I observed in Berlin, US embassy and State Department security was non-existent. As an open society, we tell or reveal to our enemies everything with one saving grace. We give away so much information that our enemies cannot process it all or don't know what to believe. Then, we get defectors from among communists, terrorists and drug dealers and they are a big help to our country.

Our ambassador often called the Pentagon in the clear and discussed classified material over the phone. When he read my reports about the firing of pro-American Dominican officers by the PRD, he told the President everything I was saying. Then the Secretary of State of the Armed Forces called me in along with other US personnel and made a speech about the situation. Who ever was informing me stopped immediately and I was told they would never work with the US embassy again. I learned that any significant information or warning passed to my ambassador or politicians in Washington was often compromised and revealed. The communists then would execute our sources while our laws against security breaches and treason were not enforced in the US. No wonder President Carter was surprised by the hostility of communists as he became a reborn observer at the end of his term in office.

One morning, as I was ready to leave for work at the embassy, I received a call from the Marine guard that we had an incident ongoing at the front gate. I checked my own house and my sentry told me that all was quiet. While driving to the embassy, I checked in with the Marine security guard on the car radio and they told me to approach the embassy carefully. The Deputy Chief of Mission, John Blacken, met me on a side street and asked if I had a gun. Having followed the ambassador's rule about not having a gun, I said I don't have a gun but I have two guns. That was fortunate because all guns were locked up in the embassy and an angry man with one or more hand grenades was at the front entrance getting ready to throw them at embassy personnel. I got my .45 caliber pistol and moved with the DCM to a spot from which we could protect the embassy and the staff trying to come to work. Before the man could throw any hand grenades, the Special Operations Battalion of the National Police arrived and killed him instantly. The incident ended as fast as it began but the ambassador was angry that a Dominican citizen was killed in front of the US embassy.

Lieutenant General Ramiro Matos Gonzalez (third from left)
with Military Attaches, Santo Domingo, 1984.

Retired military leaders in the Dominican armed forces were given a pension, aides, drivers and body guards when I was there. They held a Retired Officer's Lunch to which I was invited along with our Army Attaché. We attended the luncheon and were called to the office of the DCM afterwards where I was told that the president's staff was upset because there were rumors that I was trying to overthrow the government with the retired officers who were all supporters of former president Balaguer and the Social Christian Reformist Party (PRSC). Although I was doing my job, I was in trouble with the ambassador and he called General Goodman to complain about my help to the retired officers and supporters of former President Balaguer.

WORKING WITH BUSINESSMEN AND OTHER DUTIES

During my entire tour in the Dominican Republic, I supported the efforts of US and Dominican businessmen to maintain freedom of enterprise and implement the Caribbean Basin Initiative (CBI) against socialist pressures from leftist cabinet members and other officials. I worked closely with the general manager of ALCOA Aluminum to help the company in tough times. For working with the business community in a socialist democracy, the President of the American Chamber of Commerce presented me with a letter of commendation.

In addition, my Defense Attaché Office staff and I performed many varied administrative and operational duties. We coordinated search and rescue operations, which sometimes involved coming into the embassy to work during early morning or late night hours with US and Dominican rescue centers. We obtained communications frequency clearances for US ships and aircraft. We kept the Commandant of the Marine Corps and his staff informed through reports and informal correspondence of what was of possible interest to him.

We also assisted the Dominican government in investigative matters. After a highly publicized and nationally significant terrorist act involving a hand grenade explosion in an election center, which resulted in several voters killed and many wounded, I coordinated requests for grenade fragment analysis with US Defense and Federal Bureau of Investigation sources. I obtained the desired help for the Dominican National Police and Director of the Dominican National Intelligence service which led to the capture of the terrorists.

My office staff and I processed Dominican nominees for appointments to all US service academies and the US Merchant Marine Academy. We coordinated numerous visits by US Defense Department personnel, including that of Lieutenant General Robert Schweitzer, President of the Inter-American Defense Board in August 1983. We coordinated matters pertaining to US military personnel present in the Dominican Republic on leave or on unauthorized absence. We helped coordinate Drug Enforcement operations with the Dominican Armed Forces and the National Police laying the ground work for a Joint Armed Forces Anti-Drug Operations Center and the stationing of a US early warning radar and crew in the Dominican Republic. We coordinated hospitalization and medical treatment for Dominican militay personnel requiring US medical facilities. Finally, my office and I coordinated and cleared all US air operations involving over flight and maneuvers, as well as the projects and requirements of the Naval Oceanographic Office.

VISITING LA BARAHONA AND HAITI

During the entire time while in the Dominican Republic, I made numerous staff and liason visits to the Dominican Armed Forces. These included briefings to the Dominican General Staff, tours of the frontier with Haiti, visits to naval bases, ships, airfields, brigades and numerous battalions. I maintained excellent working relations with Lieutenant General Ramiro Matos Gonzalez, the Secretary of State of the Armed Forces, the service chiefs and the Chief of National Police. The Chief of Staff of the Army was Major General Manuel Lachapelle who was from the Cibao area of the country where they spoke Spanish with their own dialect. Upon first visiting Major General Lachapelle, he and I got along great but I could not understand fully some of the long sentences he used. Afterwards, I told Lieutenant General Matos that I felt somewhat badly that I failed to understand the long sentences fully which Major General Lachapelle used. To which General Matos, who was a very fine leader and good person said: "Dominik, don't worry we cannot understand Lachapelle either" and he told me that under Trujillo, after Lachapelle made a mistake as a duty officer, Trujillo took away his commission and sent him back to officer candidate school. I always had the highest regard for Generals Matos and Lachapelle along with the other officers and enlisted personnel. I found Admiral Olgo Santana to be another great leader and he served as the dean of the attaché corps in Washington after I departed from Santo Domingo.

In support of the Alcoa Aluminum company, I visited the Barahona area several times to visit their huge complex leased from the govenment. The ambassador was doing nothing to help the company and they wanted me to see if I could recommend any possible help from a defense standpoint. In Barahona, I reviewed the Army brigade and was invited to speak to the troops which I did. After that I ate lunch with the troops and tasted their "sancocho stew" which was excellent and served often I was told.

While checking the border, a Dominican battalion commander took me to a Haitian village where former members of the national guard lived and they wanted to salute me. During the Marine Corps occupation of Haiti they served in the national guard under Marine officers and when I arrived in the village three platoons of old men in ragged clothes were lined up and came to attention. Their senior member reported them to me as all present and accounted for. He said that they were ready for duty and he added Semper Fidelis. I said that I came on a courtesy visit and at present I did not believe that General P.X. Kelley, the Commandant of the Marine Corps required their service but I would let them know if he did. Then I was presented with a big beer bottle filled with moonshine rum and a bottle of French cognac which I brought back to the embassy and gave to John Blacken our DCM who was a great diplomat and very fine leader. I told the DCM to maybe give a swig to Richard Hines our political officer and outstanding foreign service officer.

XI INTER-AMERICAN NAVAL CONFERENCE AND EXERCISE AGILE RETRIEVAL

In close coordination with Admiral Wesley McDonald's (CINCLANT) staff in Norfolk, Virginia, my office personnel and I worked on helping Vice Admiral Arturo Borda Betances, the Chief of Staff of the Dominican Navy and his aides, to attend the XI Inter-American Naval Conference in Carthagena, Columbia. Admiral Borda received an invitation but had no assets to get him to Columbia. After the Falklands war and after President Reagan kicked the Cubans out of Grenada, the naval conference was held so that the political concerns of the Latin countries in the region could be addressed and alliances could be reaffirmed. Our acting Air Attache, a US Navy Captain, flew in from Caracas finally with his own aircraft and gave Admiral Borda with his aides a ride to Columbia and back. Admiral Borda thought the conference was important in strengthening alliances and was grateful for our help.

The Dominican Republic was less stable under President Salvador Jorge Blanco and the leftist PRD party than it was under President Joaquin Balaguer and the Social Christian Reformist Party (PRSC). Trouble was brewing on the horizon as the austerity measures imposed by President Jorge, while some PRD party members were living it up, were about to blow up into civil unrest and rioting in Santo Domingo. In anticipation of a need to evacuate American citizens, as was done during the 1965 Civil War, US Navy/Marine Corps contingency plans, along with those of the State Department, needed to be updated and made ready.

It was decided to conduct Exercise Agile Retrieval from the Headquarters US Forces Caribbean in Key West, Florida. An amphibious ready group with a US Marine battalion landing team (BLT 1/2) was sent to Key West to practice a possible evacuation and/or intervention, while John Blacken (DCM) and I were sent to Key West to provide technical advice and site specific information. I brought my maps and gave a number of briefings about how best to evacuate US citizens from the Dominican Republic recommending pretty much a repetition of what was done during the 1965 Civil War. The exercise lasted three days and was mainly a command post exercise (CPX). It was considered to be successful and very useful as a preparation for what to do if called upon to rescue or intervene in the Dominican Republic. I was commended and received a letter of appreciation from the Commander US Forces Caribbean. I was also told to stay close to the telephone if trouble started.

THE WORST RIOTS SINCE THE 1965 CIVIL WAR

In mid-April 1984, the Soviet passenger ship SS Pushkin arrived in Santo Domingo. According to my sources, KGB personnel and Cuban agents on the ship delivered money and weapons to communist party guerrilla fighters in Santo Domingo in preparation for subsequent civil unrest and riots. In combination with Soviet and Cuban support for a rebellion, the rising cost of basic necessities and uncertainty about more austerity measures led, on the anniversary of US Marine landings of 1965, during 25-29 April 1984, to four days of the worst riots since the civil war.

Despite reports from my sources that civil unrest was coming, since it was to be on the anniversary of the Marine landings of the 1965 Civil War, I knew I could take some time off and visited our Mission in Berlin. I paid a call on Colonel Roland Lejoie and talked to the officers who were doing the reconnaissance tours in East Germany. I tried to get a broader perspective on the Cold War and my own worries. I had been passed over for promotion to Colonel again and when I returned to Santo Domingo my in-basket on my desk was filled with reports of doom and gloom.

The fact that the riots were scheduled by the communists on the Marine intervention anniversary meant that it was not all about austerity and high prices. There was a connection to communist intervention in Nicaragua and El Salvador where freedom fighters were retreating because liberal Democrats in the US Congress cut their funding and passed laws prohibiting US help to anti-communists. The Cubans were sending money, arms and pro-communist volunteers into the region without any restrictions from their communist congress. Dominican pro-communist volunteers who had fought in Nicaragua and El Salvador returned to Santo Domingo to participate in the riots along with Cuban agents who were sent to act as hardcore gunmen with motorcycles against the police.

On 25 April 1984, the unrest started with many simultaneous grass fires, the burning of tires and property in Santo Domingo, and sugar fields throughout the rest of the country. At first the police was able to keep things under control without using their weapons. Then the gunmen on motorcycles drove into shopping malls, fired their guns and smashed the windows of many stores announcing that they had liberated all capitalist property for the people. They invited the people to take TV sets, computers, expensive jewelry, clothes and anything else desired because the goods had been liberated and had become the property of the people. After getting the looting started, the gunmen got on their motorcycles and disappeared. Many women, children and the elderly who were slow in looting were still in stores and store windows when the police arrived and were arrested.

Then there was a period of quiet and stand-off during which the police and armed forces hoped that the burning, looting and destruction of property would end. Upon request of our DCM, my driver and I visited the service chiefs for the first time and asked them in behalf of the ambassador not to hurt any civilians if possible. In order to call on Admiral Borda, my driver and I traveled with an M-16 and my two handguns through the deserted streets of Santo Domingo where tires and overturned cars were still burning. When I reached Admiral Borda's office, he wore a helmet and had a shotgun lying on his desk. He said: "Welcome Dominik, do you want to speak Castilliano or regular Spanish?" and a messman brought me some of their great espresso coffee. I said that our ambassador is asking please do not kill any civilians. The admiral said fine as long as they do not kill any of my sailors.

Shortly after I returned to the embassy, mobs of demonstrators appeared simultaneously in Santo Domingo as well as in the rest of the country and launched their greatest attacks so far. Then the 1st Brigade of the Dominican Army, special Dominican air force and navy units were sent into Santo Domingo from different directions. At one point, a policeman fired his handgun after his life was threatened by rioting mobs and the bullet which ricocheted off cobble stones in the road, rebounded into a line of sailors killing one of them. The sailors did not know reportedly where the bullet come from and opened up on the mob.

The rioting and unrest continued for nearly four days until the police and military brought the mobs under control. The uprising ended on 29 April and I felt that I had monitored and accurately assessed the evolution of the crisis which sparked the leftist activities and large-scale civil disturbances. My driver and I had traveled several times through riot-torn streets to personally coordinate and monitor events with each service chief and the operations center of Lieutenant General Matos, the Secretary of State of the Armed Forces. At the end of the riots, when the total numbers were assessed, 59 persons had been killed, over 400 wounded and about 4,000 were arrested. My office and I predicted the trouble in our reports and there were no surprises for which I could have been blamed. In spite of communist and Marxist socialist pressures from parts of the Salvador Jorge Blanco government and the PRD party, my office and I were able to keep the traditional pro-US and anti-communist spirit alive in the Dominican Armed Forces. There were no defections from the armed forces or police to the communists. We carried out the ambassador's orders to the letter promptly and efficiently but I had no control over the shootings and killings. Still the riots could have been worse and full blown civil war did not break out.

FAREWELL LUNCHEON HOSTED BY AMBASSADOR ANDERSON

During my entire tour in the Dominican Republic, my office personnel and I handled the processing of US Visa requests for armed forces personnel above the rank of major and lieutenant commander. This was continued even after my office first did not get a replacement for the Navy Warrant Officer/ Operations Officer and then completely lost the billet to the US Defense Attaché Office in Jamaica. The loss of the operations officer billet to Jamaica put additional work loads on me especially during ship visits.

Despite of that setback an additional port on the Atlantic Ocean side of the island was opened for US ship visits and the whole program was increased by nearly forty percent. In addition, I acted on many occasions as an embassy site officer coordinating security measures, air and land transportation, for Congressional Delegations like the entire House Ways and Means Committee and important visitors like ambassadors Jean Kirpatrick and William Middendorf.

On Wednesday 6 June 1984, a farewell cocktail/buffet was hosted by my Army Attaché in my honor and about a hundred persons came to say good by to me. On 7 June, a luncheon was hosted at the ambassadors residence by Ambassador Anderson in my honor and to bid farewell to me. Among the about forty guests, the following attended the luncheon at the ambassador's residence: Lieutenant General Ramiro Matos Gonzalez, Secretary of State of the Armed Forces, Major General Manuel Lachapelle, Assistant Secretary of State of the Armed Forces, Vice Admiral Arturo Borda Betances, Chief of the Navy, Major General Manuel Cuervo Gomes, Chief of the Army and Major General Fernando Cruz Mendez, Chief of the Air Force, along with about twenty other senior officers. The civilian guests included Ambassador Anderson, Philip Schwab the Acting DCM, Richard Hines the Political Officer, Robert Hogan the First Secretary and others.

In my brief farewell speech, I stated that I had served for nearly 28 years with two combat tours in Vietnam, a Cold War tour in East Germany and over two years in the Dominican Republic. In addition, I said that I served in the Cuban Missile Crisis, the Haiti incident, Okinawa and Korea deployments. I thanked General Matos and President Salvador Jorge Blanco, all the service chiefs, the members of the armed forces and the US embassy. I finished my remarks by saying that I was proud to have served in Santo Domingo, to have just recently contributed to the resolution of the April

1984 civil unrest and to have helped keep the spirit of freedom alive in the armed forces.

On 8 June 1984, General Matos held a farewell ceremony in his office for me during which, he presented me with a copy of Presidential Decree Number 2045 signed by President Jorge. President Jorge awarded in the decree, which I was told had been also approved by congress, the Order of Naval Merit, Second Category to me. General Matos then pinned the red, white and blue medal on my uniform and gave me a map of the Dominican Republic which he made himself with silver wire in a silver frame. He signed it in the back with appreciation for my service and my efforts of friendship towards the Dominican Republic. Just before I left, Vice Admiral Borda presented me with a ship's wheel on which the dates of my service were engraved. I was glad to have served in Santo Domingo but I was also very glad to come home.

CHAPTER 10 –
ANALYSIS AND LESSONS
LEARNED

DEALING WITH STALIN, PUTIN AND DUPLICITOUS RUSSIA

Upon return to the Pentagon, I served as a plans officer and recommended changes regarding report coordination with the State Department and about security policies. To liberal arts college educated Americans there appeared to be no threat to the outposts of freedom and America. As an immigrant, a Vietnam and Cold War veteran, I knew better. I included the lessons I learned into resource allocation and future alignment. The citation of the Meritorious Service Medal awarded to me stated that I demonstrated outstanding capabilities as a military observer and as a reporter of regional developments. The Navy and Marine Corps Overseas Service Ribbon with one star was also given to me. Last, since I was, a New York resident while on active duty, Governor George Pataki on behalf of the New York state legislature, awarded the Conspicuous Service Cross with five oak leave clusters to me. Governor Pataki wished after 9/11, that the Clinton administration had done something after the first attack on the World Trade Center, the attacks on our embassies and the USS Cole. The weapons of mass destruction used during 9/11 were box cutters, according to the governor.

Among the main lessons learned during my service, is one about dealing with the Soviets. The American desire to be trusted by Stalin blinded the Roosevelt administration to how far to believe him. I learned from my service never to trust a communist. President Roosevelt's claim that he could handle Stalin was based on the false American premise that individual friendships with the Soviets could determine national policy. Soviet leaders never operated on the basis of individual friendships. The American naiveté and trust could not have suited Stalin better who had murdered his way to power and had no respect for international law.

There is a lesson passed on to us from the KGB prisons in Vilnius, Lithuania and Potsdam, Germany which is there for everyone to see. These and other prisons have been turned into museums. The prison in Vilnius is preserved as the "Museum of Genocide Victims" and shows how easy it was for Stalin and other Communist dictators to take away freedom, justice and the right to live from innocent people. In Lithuania, between1940 and 1958, the Soviets imprisoned over 200,000 people. Many of them were disabled or died in the prisons from hard labor, starvation and disease. Another about 132,000 were deported to slave labor camps where most perished. Between 1958 and 1991, more atrocities were committed by the Soviets in Lithuania with additional thousands being sent to slave labor camps. In the KGB prison museum in Potsdam, the same brutal torture, murder and mass-deportation techniques are on display with the funding of Amnesty International.

More recently in 2006, despite the vote by Russia at the United Nation's Security Council that Iran should stop its nuclear program, reportedly Russia has continued to assist Iran with the development of laser technology to enrich uranium. Iran first admitted that it had pursued such technology but then claimed deceptively that it no longer had such a program. It is disturbing that President Vladimir Putin has demonstrated a secret willingness to aid Iran's nuclear ambitions. He has shown a disregard for the West and America while building a more assertive foreign policy in the last few years. Putin advanced his Russo-centric world-view at the G-8 Summit in St. Petersburg and helped the Arab League in its efforts to weaken support for Israel at the United Nations.

On 7 October 2006, the Russian journalist Anna Politkovskaya, known for her critical reporting of President Vladimir Putin and the war in Chechnya was murdered in her apartment building in Moscow. Prosecutors have stated that the killing could be connected to her investigtive work. Mrs. Politkovskaya has reported killings, tortures and beatings of civilians by Russian servicemen resulting in resentment and disapproval by the authorities. Russia has become one of the most dangerous places for journalists to work under President Putin. According to the Committee to Protect Journalists, at least 12 reporters have been murdered in KGB contract-style killings since Mr. Putin came to power. On 19 November 2006, Colonel Alexander Litvinenko, a former KGB officer who defected to the West, was poisoned in London in a KGB-style assassination operation. He died in the University College Hospital after being in a very serious condition for a long time. Colonel Litvinenko was an outspoken critic of the Kremlin. Lastly, on 21 October 2006, Mr. Putin announced that Russia will not support UN sanctions against Iran's nuclear program which apparently includes the development of nuclear weapons.

THE LESSONS FROM VIETNAM, KOREA AND CUBA

Another lesson learned, it seems to me, pertains to Vietnam. It has been said, that only a Harvard man such as Robert McNamara could have come up with the idea of gradually escalating the war there. Whether or not the policy of gradual escalation was conceived at the Harvard Business School, an opposing doctrine attributed to Admiral Thomas Moorer, President Ronald

Reagan, both Presidents Bush and Secretary Casper Weinberger entails the use of overwhelming force in war or none at all. Gradual escalation did not work in Vietnam and Somalia but the use of overwhelming force, when it was tried in Panama and Iraq succeeded.

A related lesson from Vietnam appears to be that politicians should not be allowed to make military decisions. Politicians in America wanted to be reelected and often refused to do the right thing in Vietnam because of communist inspired demonstrations and other leftist pressures. Even today, the season is still open on Vietnam veterans in Hollywood and the news media. In contrast to Time's Person of the Year being the American Soldier in 2004, Hollywood vilified in TNT's Word of Honor, Vietnam veterans again. TNT produced a preposterous plot in which US soldiers in Hue City in 1972 murder the French medical staff of a Red Cross hospital. In response, the lesson learned is that we need authors like B.G. Burkett, who counter such disparaging stories in his book *Stolen Valor*, in which he stated that the men who served in Vietnam are the finest troops we ever produced.

With regard to Cuba, one can learn lessons from the heroic life of Armando Valladares. He spent 22 years in Fidel Castro's prisons, according to Arnold Beichman, as a political prisoner. Valladares was one of many thousands imprisoned of which many were executed for opposing Communist ideology. Although he was not executed he was tortured, beaten, placed in isolation and subjected to sadistic experiments. According to his memoir, Valladares was locked away in the infamous tiger-cages in which he was poked with clubs so he could not sleep and he was doused regularly with the excrement of other prisoners. He was placed for years in solitary confinement and lived mired in his own waste. His unique release was obtained through an international campaign led by then French President Francois Mitterand after which Valladares wrote his memoir, "Against All Hope". A lesson learned is that left-wing politicians, journalists, special interest groups, the Carter and Clinton administrations aided and abetted the Communist enslavement of Cuba and the imprisonment of many innocent Cubans like Valladares. The United Nations also did not help.

The lesson from Korea seems to be that after Stalin was given the northern part of the country at the Yalta Conference in 1945, he and Mao Tse-tung were allowed to create a closed society under the absolute rule of a former Soviet Army major Kim IL Sung. Stalin taught Kim IL Sung how to arrest and execute people in the name of Communist ideology and how to retain absolute control. The mini-evil empire was passed on to Kim Jong IL by his father and evolved over five decades into a criminal and terrorist enterprise. The Clinton Administration believed that by appeasement the mini-evil doers would slow down or stop their bad deeds. Instead Kim Jong IL continued trafficking in narcotics, the forgery of U.S. currency, he brought down a airliner, put over 200,000 people into GULAGs (Glavnoye Upravleniye Lagerov), starved over two million people to death out of a population of 22 million, continued to develop nuclear weapons, to test them and test-fired seven long-range missiles in the direction of Japan and America on the 4th of July 2006. Dead bodies have been seen lying in the streets of Korean cities.

Hollywood has never made a movie about the whole tragedy of communism, the mass murders of whole classes and forced starvation of nations. There is a strange attraction of evil that keeps Hollywood and leftist intellectuals from facing the truth about the greatness of America and how horrible communism is. Instead of facing the truth, some in Hollywood and in the media, have produced lies and vicious anti-American propaganda. Many on the left still deny the facts of Stalin's terror, Mao's Great Leap Forward and Castro's persecution of Cuban citizens. Some activists and radical chic celebrities have combined naïve idealization of foreign dictators with a violent hatred of their own country. In my opinion, a fabricated lie that Marines killed one of their own, was made into a Broadway play called "A Few Good Men" and then made into a movie with the same name. It must be added, however, that recently one movie produced by Oliver Stone, several by Clint Eastwood and Mel Gibson have been fair, balanced and even patriotic.

The main lesson learned in Santo Domingo was that communism imported from Cuba did not help an ailing economy to recover under President Salvador Jorge Blanco. Free enterprise and freedom were needed to reactivate a faltering economy. President Joachim Balaguer returned to the presidency, shortly after I left, with electoral victories in 1986 and 1990. I like to think that I contributed to the economic stability which was recreated with the help of the Reagan administration after the Carter administration supported the PRD and brought the worst riots since the 1960s to Santo Domingo. I also believe that I helped to keep the spirit of freedom alive in the armed forces and that the Dominican Armed Forces did more to repulse Castro and communism than anyone else in the Dominican Republic.

Last, the United States Marine Corps and the US Armed Forces have played a vital role to preserve freedom and free enterprise against communism and terrorists in the world. The US has a responsibility to provide leadership against powerful dictators and their evil empires who threaten the free world and sponsor terror. Dictators have been left unchecked by liberal democrats in many countries after arguments and debates produced no action and paralysis in the end. Paralysis in the name of peace and enjoyment of the good life, resulted in nothing being done to stop the killing of many innocent women and children by mad dictators.

In the name of peace and good living, and polls which showed what the Clinton administration should do to be popular from day to day, liberals in power in America failed to act when the World Trade Center was blown up the first time. The lesson was that those who fail to learn from the past must relearn it under harsher consequences when the past repeats itself. It has been shown again and again that contrary to wishful thinking, in New York, Paris or Athens, there are actually evil and barbaric people who threaten freedom and want to destroy the free world if allowed to do so. The Democracts in Athens, in the 5th century BC, retreated into their city state and defended it until forced to wave a white flag and surrender to the enemy. The Democrats in America, want to do the same in the War on Terror, cut and run, and wave the white flag, in my opinion.

THE BATTLE FOR CUT AND RUN ON CAPITOL HILL

On 21 June 2006, defense spending legislation was before the U.S. Senate and Senators presented their views on the Global War on Terror. Some Democratic Senators wanted a schedule for withdrawal from Iraq with specific time lines to which Republican Senators objected. Senator Chuck Hagel said that he was in Congress during April 1975 along with Representative Jack Murtha when all spending for the Republic of Vietnam was terminated. Senator Hagel said that it was terrible to watch when the Communists were given a free hand to mass-murder and enslave many innocent people in Vietnam.

On about 20 June 2006, the remains of soldiers--PFC Kristian Menchaca, of Huston and PFC Thomas Tucker, of Madras, Oregon, -- were recovered near a power plant in the town of Yusufia, where they had been operating a vehicle check point that came under attack. The two soldiers reportedly had been tortured and beheaded by the terrorists. Senators Leahy, Levin, Durbin, Kerry and other Democrats were blaming the Bush administration first and not the terrorists for the problems in Iraq. These senators offered nothing but criticism and obstruction. They also wanted a rapid withdrawal from Iraq or "cut and run" leaving the terrorists free to mass-murder and establish a victorious international gangster state in Iraq.

With a terrorist state established in Iraq, the suicide bombers would be free to consolidate their power and expand. They would travel to more and more places in the world for attacks and destruction. Senator George Allen stated that our country needs to be united against those who want to kill and destroy us. We should not be giving, according to Senator Allen, hope to the terrorists that we will cut and run as we did in Somalia and Vietnam. It seems short sighted to abandon our friends and allies in time of war. Also, avoiding confrontations with terrorists only emboldens them and gives them opportunities to organize and plan more evil deeds. If we give in to the political ground swell from a segment of our society which is against the President Bush domestic agenda and we run from the terrorists, we may return to the policies which would have us tolerate occasional bombings and attacks in our country, with the loss of a few thousand friends and family members here or there, until we are possibly subjugated by Islamic totalitarians.

THE "NATION" MAGAZINE TRADITION OF BLAME AMERICA FIRST

In early July 2006, Iran's proxy war to destroy Israel escalated into Hezbollah rocket attacks from Lebanon against villages and cities. When Israel retaliated, the editors of the most influential and oldest left-wing American magazine the "Nation" published a lead article condemning Israel as a terrorist state and blamed the war itself on Israel's occupation of Arab territories. The "Nation's" editors' support and apologetics for Communism and radical Islamic fanatics is a continuation of a long tradition of aiding and abetting the totalitarian enemies of America and the West.

For almost a century, the editors of the "Nation" justified and articulated every Communist tyrant from Stalin and Mao Tse-tung to Castro and Kim Jong Il. After the 9/11 attack, the editors of the "Nation" decried America's "empire" and "jingoism". They characterized America as a "terrorist state", according to David Horowitz. They opposed the overthrow of Saddam Hussein and continued to oppose the liberation of Iraq as an "imperialist occupation".

One editor of the "Nation" appeared several times on a television program on MSNBC, hosted by Chris Matthews, to blame America first and not the radical Islamic fanatics. The programs were designed to propagate anti-Americanisms and repeatedly denigrated the service of our troops around the world and at home. During World War II, it seems to me that the fifth column activities of MSNBC activists would not have been tolerated which have taken place during the War on Terror. Another American reporter by the name of Matthews, who supported left-wing causes for decades was called by Fidel Castro, "a useful tool".

NEWS COVERAGE OF THE WAR ON TERROR IN IRAQ OFTEN MISSES PROGRESS AND SUCCESSES

The Department of Defense public affairs staff and military combat correspondents, according to Major N. F. Murphy, a Public Affairs Officer, worked hard to get the latest news out to the American people about the War on Terror in Iraq and Afghanistan. Unfortunately, members of the press often do not work as hard and miss what positive steps are taken and the context of casualties. Successes and progress in Iraq have not made the headlines often in the mainstream media any more since the time of the spectacular victory by American and Coalition Forces which culminated in the pulling down of the statue of Saddam Hussein in Baghdad.

A major decline in the collective media reporting began with the mass exodus of embedded reporters, from units with which they embarked from Kuwait, after Baghdad was secured. Shortly after the various statues of Saddam Hussein were pulled down, many reporters "disembedded" and set up office in Baghdad hotels. Soon, instead of living and working with Marines and soldiers, the press switched to quick in and out visits, as short as a few days, then preparing their reports from Baghdad hotels. In early 2003, about 85 percent of the embedded reporters left their units and set up shop in hotels. Then many reporters relied on second and third-hand information and paid Iraqi "stringers" to gather for them media desired stories and take photographs that would sell at home. This practice has been continued to the present. Reporting quality has dropped slowly, from indepth coverage across Iraq and many units performing in a superb manner, as mainstream media outlets largely ignored them and their significant progress.

In 2005, a major disservice, according to Major Murphy, took place during a media offensive to mark the 2,000th casualty in Iraq, during which the press created many casualty count news headlines and discredited the sacrifice of the brave Marines and soldiers who were doing the fighting. Instead of reporting about significant achievements like the constitutional referendum or reconstruction, the press focused on the 2,000th member killed in action, while omitting each and every person's sacrifice for our country and the American people. There is no greater love than giving one's life for your country, freedom, justice and life for millions of the oppressed. There was no difference between the first KIA or the 2,000th except for purposes of media hype and frenzy.

Lance Corporal Britton Warfield kneeling in the center of
the bottom row, 1st Platoon, Company C, 3rd Marines,
"Operation Mountain Lion", Afghanistan, 2006.

Most media organizations have continued the hype about the rising death toll and have combined casualty reports with suicide bombing, falling presidential approval ratings, prisoner abuse allegations and "blame America first" stories often made up with little factual evidence to support them. This kind of news coverage has negated the achievement of Iraq's constitution and the creation of a free democratic government, while providing fodder for shameful political rhetoric, protests and opposition at the expense of brave Marines and soldiers who are fighting against fanatical terrorists and ruthless murderers.

Few media outlets have taken the time to examine the continued sacrifice of our military to our nation. These brave servicemen stand for the highest ideals and deserve better coverage of their accomplishments. Our media often unwittingly provide aid to our enemies by seeking interviews and freely showing videos of terrorist deeds and statements. The terrorists who show no mercy or compassion are allowed by our media to do any crime or travesty without adverse publicity but our servicemen must have their hands tied behind their back or our media will produce headlines and hype about their conduct. The hype stories are often magnified by some television programs such as those on MSNBC and CNN which are often vicious and anti-American, in my opinion, with no loyalty to our country.

FAILED NEWS AND MAINSTREAM MEDIA COVERAGE OF OPERATION IRAQI FREEDOM

According to Major Murphy, the news and mainstream media reporting has failed to provide meaningful coverage of Operation Iraqi Freedom. Many media conglomerates continue to produce news based on artificial ideas and imagined time lines. They concentrate on sporadic attacks and the smallest incident if it is adverse to the American and the Coalition Forces military. If it bleeds it leads and anything positive for America is not news.

In newspapers like the Washington Post and the New York Times, events are embellished and bent to fit the policy line of our Democratic Party. The minutest misdeeds of our military are sensationalized whereas enemy murderers are given a free pass when they decapitate and torture the innocent. Pictures of the same Improvised Explosive Device (IED) are sometimes shown repeatedly in newspapers and on television to scare women, children and the elderly, so that they would want to wave the white flag and cut and run. Then politicians use the Washington Post and the New York Times as a primary source for allegations against the American military no matter how dubious the newspaper story may be. The more outrageous the story the better it sells: (1) on Capitol Hill to the anti-war politicians, (2) the American Civil Liberties

Union (ACLU), (3) berserk peace activists and associated religious groups, and (4) the seven retired general officers who out of about 7,500 retired general/admirals are anti-war protesters, just like Jane Fonda, Senator John Kerry and some others were during the Vietnam War.

According to some widely publicized articles, if Senator John Kerry had been elected president, he would have been the first commander in chief whose photograph has been honored by a one-time enemy, Communist Vietnam, and continues to be honored, in gratitude for helping to defeat America and the Republic of Vietnam during the longest war in our history. A photograph of Senator Kerry meeting with victorious Communist leaders in 1983, hangs in the War Remnants Museum in Saigon (now Ho Chi Minh City). According to the best-selling book "Unfit for Command", the wing of the museum which honors Senator Kerry, is dedicated to Americans who helped the North Vietnamese defeat the Republic of Vietnam and throw the US Armed Forces out of Vietnam. A 1974 Vietnamese Communist Party report is quoted on a display in the museum: "we would like to thank the communist parties and working class of the countries of the world ....and progressive human beings for their whole hearted support and strong encouragement to our people's patriotic resistance against the U.S. for national salvation". A separate women's museum display contains a photograph of Jane Fonda meeting with Viet Cong Foreign Minister Madame Nguyen Thi Binh.

Just as was the case in the past in Vietnam, during the War on Terror, there is a media war going on parallel to the shooting war. Combat correspondents and military media relations officers try to provide the public with first hand news and information on which to base sound judgments, while most journalists search for any sensational story that may mean the end of the war or garner a Pulitzer Prize. In turn, the Pulitzer Prize is awarded by an apparently biased committee for anti-American news stories like the revelation that there are U.S. prison camps overseas or similar "got-cha" articles which blame America first for often unfounded and overinflated Madison Avenue allegations like the "Zippo Lighter Incident", the false claim reported on CNN that U.S. Special Forces used deadly chemical agents in combat in Vietnam and the false Newsweek magazine allegation that prison guards at Guantanamo Bay flushed a copy of the Koran down a toilet.

Apparently Newsweek owned by the Washington Post eagerly propagates any possible bad news about the War on Terror alleged by liberals in politics, disgruntled government employees or others. For example, the Washington Post, New York Times and other liberal media, fell for and carried lie after lie about the White House for three years on their front pages, for a charlatan and small time ambassador Joseph Wilson. Wilson's wife was not a covert agent. After three years, of demagoguery and public scandal during which Wilson had a good time and Carl Rowe took the heat, the embarrassing facts became known. Wilson and his wife filed a purely political lawsuit anyway and it was still disseminated by the liberal media with no retractions or apology.

Reportedly Osama Bin Laden created a media and public affairs organization a decade ago to produce propaganda press releases, videos and interviews. Since 9/11, it can be seen that there has been a global media war conducted by the terrorists, with some foreign media acting as spokesmen for the terrorists and hostile governments. Unfortunately our liberal media have been duped into participating to various degrees in the propaganda against our country. The Washington Post, New York Times, CNN, MSNBC and CBS in particular, joined the terrorists in anti-American propaganda by replaying their press releases while adding commentary that we need a time table for withdrawal from Iraq and we should never have been there in the first place. Our media have been joined by politicians like Senator Harry Reid who repeated Congressman Jack Murtha's claims and demands that we withdraw immediately. According to Dan Bartlett, Counselor to President George W. Bush, our enemies are doing a better job of communicating than we are. Media propaganda is central to the struggle we are facing in the War on Terror, as it was during the Vietnam War.

According to Bartlett, if we pull our forces out of the Middle East the terrorists will not leave us alone but will follow us to our homes. Bartlett stated on television, that some Democrats have not helped the war effort or our Armed Forces by calling President Bush a liar and accusing him of fighting the wrong war. In my opinion, Bartlett has been a better counselor to President Bush during the War on Terror than John Dean was to President Richard Nixon during the Vietnam War. To this day, after being fired by President Nixon, Dean has continued to be disgruntled and defeatist, it seems to me. Other lawyers, like the ones belonging to the trial lawyers lobby, have conducted class-action warfare against corporate America recovering over $45 billion and becoming the Democratic Party's most generous supporters. A leading class-action law firm, Millberg Weiss, has been recently charged in a 20-count indictment with obstruction of justice, perjury, bribery and fraud, despite support from Democratic Congressmen Charles Rangel, Gary Ackerman and Robert Wexler. According to Bartlett, we have to carefully consider the consequences of careless rehtoric, the recommendations for bad decisions in the Middle East and how they are going to play out.

Recently A U.S. Senator said it best on the Senate floor, in my opinion, we have been at war with the terrorists for over twenty years yet our Democratic Party members ignored the terrorists in the past and want to continue to ignore them in the future despite repeated attacks against us, to include the second attack against our World Trade Center on 9/11 which cost about three thousand lives. Some Democrats want to fight against the While House and the Pentagon instead of the terrorists. In my opinion, we should unite and figure out how to win instead of fighting each other. Perhaps a cliche applies to us, that united we stand and divided we fall. If we continue divided we will probably not fall but we will have a much harder time, fighting against the terrorists and supporting our troops, who are risking their lives in combat for us. Our Armed Forces deserve our full support in combat and deserve better than personal agendas, partisanship, misinformation, defeatism, along with all kinds of intentional or unintentional aid and comfort to the enemy.

On 8 October 2006, in the Outlook Section of the Washington Post, Robert Dallek wrote an article, "It's Time for Him to Go" and Stanley Karnow wrote one, "Worse Than McNamara?" with both articles displayed in a section titled "Rumsfeld Watch". In my opinion, the Washington Post reporters and editors were out of line and in a "state of denial" about the victories and successes in the War on Terror. Apparently, the ad hominem attacks against Secretary of Defense Donald H. Rumsfeld at election time were motivated by politics and the desire to defeat Republicans running for office. In my opinion, our Armed Forces and civilian leaders have done an outstanding job in the Middle East and America is safer thanks to them. We owe a great deal of thanks to Secretary Rumsfeld, the British Prime Minister Toni Blair and President George W. Bush for their great leadership and vision in the War on Terror. Tactics may change in the War on Terror but the goal to keep the free world safe will remain the same.

In late November 2006, Brent Bozell stated in a speech before the National Press Club that in twentyfive years of watching the national media he never saw before the kind of one-sided, distorted and vicious news coverage as that of the November 2006 elections. He said that members of the national press should be ashamed of themselves for parroting the talking points of the Democrats and becoming complete spokespersons for the Democratic Party. The editors and staff of the Washington Post, inserted themselves into the political campaigns in Maryland and Virginia, in my opinion, with onesided hype and vicious rehtoric against the Republican candidates, the Armed Forces, the Secretary of Defense and the President of the United States badly damaging our war efforts and the defense of our country against terrorists and other enemies. In effect, after losing 2,865 KIA and about 21,000 WIA in three years of fighting and accomplishing most objectives of the War on Terror while on the way to completing more, the national media have hyped defeat. Many in the socialist media declared that we have lost the War on Terror despite keeping our country safe for five years, eliminating in Iraq the spring board for suicide bombers and confronting the terrorists on their own ground successfully.

On 20 October 2006, Congressman Duncan Hunter, Chairman of the Armed Forces Committee, told Secretary Rumsfeld to deny CNN reporters the privilege of going to our combat units for information because CNN took film footage from the enemy and became a publicist for the terrorists. CNN exploited the death of a U.S. soldier due to sniper fire by showing the enemy film on CNN news. By showing the enemy propaganda in its news program, CNN intentionally offered aid and comfort to the enemy, in my opinion, instead of serving our country and the American people. According to a well known commentator, Lieutenant Colonel Oliver North USMC (Ret), the socialist media like CNN are determining a negative view of the War on Terror for the American people while using taxpayer paid for public assets for broadcasting. They grieve, like we all do, for the tragic loss of a Marine, sailor, soldier or airman in combat with good justification but they neglect to point out that we have in the War on Terror the lowest casualty rate of any war we ever fought. Also, for about five years no major buildings in America, no embassies, troop living quarters like the one in Saudi Arabia or ships like the USS Cole have been damaged or destroyed.

Last, it should be mentioned that we have to thank Pope John Paul II for speaking out, resisting and exposing the horrors of Communism and the evil empire. He and President Ronald Reagan led the fight against Communism and prevailed. It has now been confirmed by the Italian government, that Chairman Leonid Brezhnev of the Communist Party of the Soviet Union ordered the KGB to assiassinate the Pope. However, John Paul II survived the attempted murder after he was badly wounded and continued to fight for freedom. Budapest, the capital of Hungary, recently paid tribute to Ronald Reagan's fight against Communism with a sculpture of the former U.S. president in the popular city park. Hopefully, Pope Benedict XVI who leads about one billion followers will continue to speak out and expose the terrorists for what they are. They bring horror and mayhem, blow up innocent women and children and decapitate journalists.

A BRIGHT FUTURE AHEAD

Despite the domination of politics by the liberal press and media, on 7 November 2006, American voters gave the Democrats only a small majority in the House and a razor-thin majority in the Senate. Many voters were convinced by the socialist media that we were losing the War on Terror and that there were gay, racist and corrupt persons among the Republicans but not among the Democrats. Probably that is why the Iranian leaders called the election a victory for Iran. Al Qaeda, with the support of the Washington Post and many Democrats, proclaimed victory in Iraq despite contrary testimony by General John Abizaid, our Commander in Iraq, who said that he did not need or want anymore U.S. troops. Last, Mexico demanded after the election, that the White House in view of the new Democratic majority government, grant amnesty to all illegal immigrants.

The Democrats and socialist media did not mention during the election campaign some harsh realities which President Bush and Republicans like Congressman Duncan Hunter were working hard to overcome. First, North Korea and Iran have continued to become nuclear powers, with verbal outrage, but no action from the United Nations. Second, long before "9/11" and the consequent War on Terror, extremist Islamic groups have killed many Americans around the world and will continue to try to do so, while the Democrats wish it were not so and advocate retreat. Third, many liberals and independents in the United States, have continued to believe that China and Russia have been our allies when history has shown that they have obstructed almost every recent United States initiative or policy. Last, given the bad foreign policy record of the Democrats, it seems that they must come up with a good plan to win the War on Terror, similar to the one President Bush already has, for a bright future and work with the Republicans to make it happen.

After coming to New York as a small immigrant child from Lithuania, I spent my whole life fighting Communism during the Cold War. The Cold War was won when the Wall in Berlin came down and the Soviet Union collapsed from the weight of its own corruption and evil. On 30 April 2004, I watched midshipmen help raise the Lithuanian and European Union flags at the Lithuanian Embassy in Washington, D.C., as Lithuania and nine other nations became full members of the European Union and NATO. Lithuania became a strong ally in the war on terror and has sent troops to Iraq, Afghanistan, Kosovo and Georgia.

For many people the Vietnam war is over but for me and those who fought there it will never be over. We did our job, fought for the right reasons and won the war. Then Congress abandoned Vietnam and lost the peace. Since then, many old communist hardliners in Hanoi have died. The younger leaders know that they have to allow free trade and democracy or their government will collapse like the Soviet Union.

In Latin America, Fidel Castro with his Communist heirarchy and radical socialist Hugo Chavez, along with the Sao Paulo Forum, are still conducting an anti-American campaign that will ally itself with Middle East terrorists or anyone else bent on attacking the U.S. Reportedly radical Islamic terrorists have been trained in Venezuela to speak Spanish to be able to blend into the U.S. population as hispanic immigrants. But many drug dealers, thugs and terrorists are being brought to justice.

Lithuanian soldiers serving in Iraq under Joint Command, 2004.

An international coalition of over 30 nations has supported the U.S. in Iraq and stands with America in the cause of freedom. In Iraq, the dictator and his sons will never torment the people again. In Afghanistan, the people made a successful transition to self-government and are building a free nation. About 50 million people have been freed as a result of confronting the enemy on his own territory.

Despite serious challenges significant progress has been made in the war on terror. Law enforcement and the courts are not being used as the primary tools to oppose terror. Instead, U.S. Marines and the U.S. Armed Forces have taken the fight to the enemy and the U.S. is more secure. The American people can be proud of what has been achieved. The Armed Forces have acted with restraint and measured response toward terrorists and with decency towards innocent people. There is cause for optimism as the U.S. and the Middle East will be safer, free and prosperous in the future. Our friends know that they can trust, and our enemies know that they must fear, America's decisive leadership in the cause of freedom and justice for all.

EPILOGUE

In early September 2004, I visited Lithuania after many years. The new generation is prospering and is free from communism. The economy is growing by seven percent per year. The KGB Museum in Vilnius is crowded with tourists instead of innocent people who during the Soviet occupations were tortured and executed there. The Gediminas Prospect street is filled with upscale stores, restaurants and outdoor cafes. The townhall has the words of President George W. Bush on its wall about freedom and the support for freedom by the United States of America in the world.

The Old Town of Vilnius is one of Europe's most attractive town centers. With its cobblestone streets and beautiful facades, it offers a view into the past. Lithuania is undergoing a rapid transition from being a captive nation of the Soviet Union to a free and vibrant member of the European Union and NATO. The future looks finally great for the Baltic States because of America's leadership and support for their right to be free.

President George W. Bush and President Valdas Adamkus
in Vilnius in November 2002.

During late September 2005, I visited Lithuania again and was happy to see the progress being made. At the same time, in an apparent test of Lithuanian airspace, a Russian Air Force SU-25 fighter-bomber was sent to overfly Lithuania but crashed due to engine malfunction. The pilot ejected safely but was detained by Lithuanian authorities. The incident indicated to me that Russian-Lithuanian relations are good on the surface but can be strained rapidly.

In early 2006, Vice President Dick Cheney paid a visit to Lithuania on the way to Moscow and his remarks about freedom and justice were greatly appreciated by the people of Lithuania and other states in the region. Also, I noted during my visits, that the Lithuanian people are forever grateful to President George W. Bush for his words in Vilnius on 23 November 2002, which are engraved on the State Council Building: "Anyone who would choose Lithuania as an enemy has also made an enemy of the United States of America". I was told that many Lithuanians cried after hearing the words of President Bush and his kind gesture.

May God bless our Marines, sailors, soldiers and airmen who are fighting to protect freedom, justice and the free world against terrorists and communists in our wars overseas and at home. May God bless our President, the American people and our country. May the American people unite and figure out how to help our troops to win in combat, instead of partisanship, propagating personal agendas and fighting at home with each other. May there be no wretched capitulation to the enemy and not another Saigon evacuation with people hanging on to helicopters to escape. Semper Fidelis.

SOURCES AND BIBLIOGRAPHY

The primary sources used were as follows:

(1) Nargele, Dominik, Personal Papers, Award citations, Orders and Photographs, 1945 to 2004.

(2) Nargele, Dominik, <u>Vietnam Diary</u>, 1965-1966, Volume I and II, Vietnam, Unpublished.

(3) Nargele, Dominik, <u>From Immigrant to U.S. Marine</u>, Xlibris Corporation, Philadelphia, 2005.

The secondary sources used were as follows:

(1) Allard, D.C., <u>Caribbean Tempest</u>, Naval Historical Center, Department of the Navy, Washington, DC, 1990, pp. 2-3, pp. 24-47.

(2) Allied Museum, <u>Mission Accomplished</u>, Berlin, 2004, p. 101, a photograph of my reconnaissance vehicle is shown.

(3) Beevor, Anthony, <u>The Fall of Berlin 1945</u>, Viking Press, London 2002. pp. 17-135

(4) Beichman, Arnold, "Viva Valladares", <u>The Washington Times</u>, Washington, DC, July 9, 2006, p. B3.

(5) Buckley, William F., <u>The Fall of the Berlin Wall</u>, University Press of Kansas, Wichita 2004, pp. 7-97.

(6) Fahey, John A., <u>Licensed To Spy</u>, Naval Institute Press, Annapolis, Maryland 2002, pp. 91-105.

(7) Grathwol, Robert P. and Moorhus, Donita M., <u>American Forces In Berlin, Cold War Outpost</u>, Department of Defense, Legacy Resource Management Program, Cold War Project, Washington, DC, 1994, pp. 156.

(8) Horowitz, David, "Left History", <u>The Washington Times</u>, 20 July 2006, p. A2.

(9) Karnow, Stanley, <u>Vietnam</u>, Penguin Books, New York, New York, 1983, pp. 28-31.

(10) Kirk, Richard, "The Weatherman Above Ground", <u>American Spectator Online</u>, www.spectator.org, 12 June 2006.

(11) Murphy, N.F., "If It Bleeds, It Leads," <u>Follow Me</u>, Camp Lejeune, NC, July 2006, pp. 30-31

(12) Museum of Genocide Victims, <u>Pamphlet for Tenth Anniversary</u>, Vilnius, 2002, pp. 1-6.

(13) Barone, Michael, "Our Covert Enemies", The Washington Times, Washington, DC, 22 August 2006, p. A14.

(14) Morris, Amy, "The Prevailing Evil in the World", <u>The Northern Virginia Sun</u>, 31 October 1997, pp. 15.

(15) Nargele, Dominik, <u>Looking Back At The Intervention in the Dominican Republic in 1965</u>, Paper for Foreign Service Institute, Unpublished, 1982, pp. 1-12.

(16) Neiber, Comrade Lieutenant General, "MfS Handwritten Note", <u>Main Division VIII</u>, Berlin, 26 March 1985.

(17) Simmons, E.H., <u>The Marines in Vietnam 1954-1973</u>, History and Museums Divison, Headquarters, US Marine Corps, Washington, DC., 1974, pp. 26-122

(18) USAF Historical Division, <u>Historical Analysis of the 14-15 February 1945 Bombings of Dresden</u>, Pentagon, Washington, DC 2004, pp. 1-20.

(19) United States Department of State, <u>Human Rights In The USSR</u>, An Informal Research Study, Washington, DC, 1983, pp. 1-3